YORK NOTES

General Editors: Professor A.N. Jeffares (*University of Stirling*) & Professor Suheil Bushrui (*American University of Beirut*)

Muriel Spark

THE PRIME OF MISS JEAN BRODIE

Notes by Trevor Royle
(MA, FRSE)

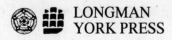**LONGMAN
YORK PRESS**

YORK PRESS
Immeuble Esseily, Place Riad Solh, Beirut

LONGMAN GROUP LIMITED
Longman House, Burnt Mill,
Harlow, Essex CM20 2JE, England
Associated companies, branches and representatives
throughout the world

First published 1995

ISBN 0–582–26243–7

Phototypeset by Gem Graphics, Trenance, Mawgan Porth, Cornwall
Printed in Singapore

Contents

Part 1

Introduction

The life and works of Muriel Spark

Muriel Sara Camberg was born in Edinburgh in 1918. Her father, a mechanical engineer, came from a Scottish-Jewish family, while her mother, who had been a music teacher before her marriage, was English – from Watford in Hertfordshire – and a Presbyterian. Muriel had one brother, five years her elder. In her autobiography, *Curriculum Vitae* (1992), she describes her childhood as an orderly, polite, even prosaic existence, which was much enlivened by the Jewish relatives on her father's side, while her mother's 'Englishness' – her English turns of phrase and dress – was often a source of embarrassment to her, at an age when girls are desperate to conform.

She was educated at one of Edinburgh's best-known schools, the James Gillespie's High School for Girls – the model for the Marcia Blaine School in *The Prime of Miss Jean Brodie*. Muriel Spark has described her twelve years there as 'the most formative years of my life, and in many ways the most fortunate for a future writer'. Its pupils were from almost every religion: Catholic, Jewish, Episcopalian, Presbyterian, Hindu; tolerance prevailed, although with a distinctly puritanical slant. At the age of eleven, Muriel Spark writes in her autobiography, she fell under the spell of one of the teachers there – Miss Christina Kay – who inspired her with her accounts of foreign travel and her interest in music and art. (Miss Kay, although a deeply devout woman, would later be the inspiration for the character of Miss Brodie herself.) At school Muriel began to write poetry.

When she left at seventeen, she attended the Heriot Watt College to complete her education. This college taught a more scientific approach to the English language, and Muriel took a course in précis-writing (the influence of which is very much apparent in her economical, unpretentious, direct prose).

In order to be able to write, which is what Muriel had already decided she wanted to do, she felt she had first to 'live'. She loved going to dances with her brother, and having obtained a teaching post in a small private school, she learnt shorthand and typing, which enabled her to take a job as secretary in a very elegant women's department store in Edinburgh.

With many of her friends marrying, in 1937 she too decided to marry. Her choice was a teacher, Sydney Oswald Spark, some thirteen years her senior, and she went to live with him in Southern Rhodesia. The marriage however was a difficult one, and Muriel found living in the colonies too much like English provincial life: too lazy and too slow. After two years in Africa and the birth of her son, she decided to divorce. War had broken out and return to Britain was impossible, but eventually in 1944 she managed to make her way home on a troop ship in very dangerous circumstances.

She settled in the Kensington area of London, and was lucky enough to find a job with the Foreign Office in their Political Intelligence Department which dealt with propaganda and psychological warfare intended to deceive the enemy. After the war she worked as General Secretary of the Poetry Society editing the *Poetry Review* from 1947 to 1949, and working in a small publishers' offices in South Kensington. This London period of the late 1940s and early 1950s forms the setting to a number of her early novels: *The Girls of Slender Means* (1963) which features the women's club she stayed in just north of Kensington Gardens and a publisher's office; *The Comforters* (1957), and later novels such as *Loitering with Intent* (1981) and *A Far Cry from Kensington* (1988) which hark back to those early days.

In 1954 she converted to Roman Catholicism. Since then she has lived in Rome, New York and Tuscany, and her later novels have frequently been associated with the English Catholic tradition in fiction.

Her first work as a writer concentrated on poetry and biography – she wrote reassessments of Mary Shelley, John Masefield and (with Derek Stanford) Emily Brontë – but she turned to fiction after winning a short-story competition organised by the *Observer* newspaper. Her first novel *The Comforters* was followed by a number of novels which examine the moral ambiguities inherent in the main characters, most notably Mrs Pettigrew in *Memento Mori* (1959), Dougal Douglas in *The Ballad of Peckham Rye* (1960) and Patrick Seton in *The Bachelors* (1961). Their diablerie suggests a vision of the devil as a terrible human familiar who is also a figure of fun.

Later novels mix satire with reality and introduce a new element of social criticism. *The Abbess of Crewe* (1974), for example, is a sustained allegory about the Watergate scandal which destroyed the US President Richard Nixon as well as being a satirical fantasy about ecclesiastical politics; and *Territorial Rights* (1979) is as much about the prevalence of international terrorism as it is about the macabre notion that everyone has something criminal to hide.

With the exception of *The Mandelbaum Gate* (1965), a lengthy work which follows the heroine Barbara Vaughan's quest for her own identity and involves the trial of the Nazi Adolf Eichmann, Spark's novels are generally short and elegantly written. The property of the fable or parable is never far away: *The Girls of Slender Means* begins with the fairytale words 'Long ago . . .' and *Not to Disturb* (1971) contains a gallery of characters from the Gothic tradition.

Her most recent novels include *The Only Problem* (1984), *A Far Cry from Kensington* (1988) and *Symposium* (1991). Amongst her collections are *Collected Poems* (1967), *Collected Stories* (1968) and *The Stories of Muriel Spark* (1987). Her autobiography, *Curriculum Vitae*, was published in 1992.

She became a Dame of the British Empire (DBE) in 1993 and amongst other awards she has received the Italia Prize, the James Tait Black Memorial Prize, the FNAC Prix Etranger, the Saltire Prize and the Ingersoll T. S. Eliot Award. She was elected an honorary member of the American Academy of Arts and Letters in 1978 and L'Ordre des Arts et des Lettres in France in 1988.

Although much of Muriel Spark's work has been set outside her native Scotland, some in actual geographical locations, others in places which seem to be as much her own creation, she has explained the importance to her artistic growth of her childhood spent in Edinburgh in her essay 'What Images Return' (1970). From her Edinburgh experience came her sixth novel, *The Prime of Miss Jean Brodie* (1961) a penetrating study of the dynamics of Calvinism, set in an Edinburgh girls' school.

Muriel Spark and Scotland

In 'What Images Return', she gave expression to her 'cautious, affectionate, critical' appreciation of Edinburgh, a recognition that was heightened by her sense of acceptance by it and its people: 'it is the place where I was first understood'.

Edinburgh also impressed itself on her imagination by its ancient beauty and unexpected city-scapes, by the sheer perpendicularity of it all. In spite of its tendency to take a fierce delight in puritanical virtues – a drawback which she characterised as the 'nevertheless' principle, the careful balancing of opposites – she enjoyed 'the informed air of the place, its haughty and remote anarchism'. To use her own 'nevertheless' principle, Muriel Spark, having both a Scottish and Jewish inheritance, has lived most of her life abroad and has written only one distinctly Scottish novel; nevertheless, she is a novelist with a peculiarly Scottish frame of mind. She acknowledges the influence that her Edinburgh childhood has had on her writing and in the same essay describes herself as 'a writer of Scottish formation' whose literary career has been indelibly stamped by being born and educated in Scotland.

That questioning of the validity of a writer's national identity is peculiar to the peoples of small nations, especially when they themselves are unsure who they really are, or who they might become. The English, with several centuries of Empire-building behind them, tend to assume that anyone writing in the English language can be considered one of them, that Englishness can be conferred on them by a process of assimilation.

Not so the Scots, who take a greater degree of interest in the claims of nationality; as a result Scottish writers, especially novelists, are tested more thoroughly in the incontrovertible Scottishness of their work.

There is an identifiable and strong Scottish literary tradition, exemplified at its best by the writings, after 1603, of Allan Ramsay, Robert Fergusson, Robert Burns, Walter Scott, Robert Louis Stevenson and Hugh MacDiarmid, and also by the work of a variety of poets, novelists, dramatists, historians, diarists and essayists; but it is a tradition beset by self-doubts and questionings about whether it is indeed a tradition.

Since Muriel Spark has claimed that Edinburgh has had a noticeable effect on her mind, prose style and ways of thought, it is fruitful to examine her sense of Scottishness in relationship to her Edinburgh novel, *The Prime of Miss Jean Brodie*. (In his study of Muriel Spark, Karl Malkoff found her mixed Jewish and Presbyterian parentage and her Presbyterian education 'an unlikely beginning for one of England's more important contemporary novelists'.)

The Prime of Miss Jean Brodie is set in Edinburgh during the 1930s and on one level it contains one of the best portraits drawn of the city, a picture devoid of the trap of romanticism into which so many Scottish novelists have fallen.

Edinburgh is also seen as a city of contrasts, at once 'a European capital, the city of Hume and Boswell' (p. 43), and yet 'a foreign country which intimates itself by its new smells and shapes and its new poor' (p. 32). But it is the delineation of Edinburgh as a dark and sombre place that is such a telling counterpoint to the creation of its main character, Miss Jean Brodie, the monstrous teacher of susceptible young girls at the Marcia Blaine School. Edinburgh is seen through 'the haunted November twilight' (p. 20), and Jean Brodie herself has a suitably dark lineage: 'I am a descendant, do not forget, of Willie Brodie, a man of substance' (p. 88).

Deacon William Brodie is one of Edinburgh's most famous historical characters, a man whose exploits have become part of the city's mythology. By placing her heroine within his family lineage, Muriel Spark was doing more than just adding local colour. Brodie was a man who led two lives: a town councillor by day who held the post of Deacon of Wrights and Masons, he led a gang of burglars by night and held the city within a reign of terror.

His come-uppance was due to over-reaching. He bungled a robbery in the General Excise Office in the Canongate and was forced to flee to Holland. Through a series of accidents and betrayals he was arrested, returned to Scotland and hanged on a gallows which he himself had designed in happier times. Edinburgh had been scandalised by his actions, but the myth lived on and the story of Deacon Brodie became one of the city's most potent legends: a man who led a life of contradictions.

That sense of secret alienation from society while at the same time claiming public allegiance to its morality is a recognisable feature of Scottish society. Robert Louis Stevenson used Deacon Brodie as a partial source for his novel *The Strange Case of Dr Jekyll and Mr Hyde* (1886), in which the central character, Dr Henry Jekyll, haunted by the consciousness of a double identity within himself, experiments with a drug which will separate his identity into good and evil. In that guise evil is allowed to rule and Hyde begins to commit a number of crimes, culminating in a murder. Increasingly unable to control his metamorphoses, Jekyll finds Hyde becoming the dominant character, and to save himself from public exposure is forced to take his own life.

James Hogg's *The Private Memoirs and Confessions of a Justified Sinner* (1824), a novel of diabolic possession, theological satire and local legend, is a more complete illustration of the same theme. The story, set in the years immediately prior to the Act of Union between Scotland and England of 1707, concerns two brothers, George Colwan, the son of a laird, and Robert, who is supposed to be the illegitimate son of his mother's spiritual adviser, the Rev. Robert Wringhim. The brothers, who grow up apart, are always in conflict when they meet, and when George is murdered, Robert is suspected of fratricide and disappears. This novel also expresses the theme of predestination, which is echoed in *The Prime of Miss Jean Brodie*, namely that sins committed by an 'elect and justified person' cannot imperil the hope of salvation. Robert has reached this conclusion from the narrow Calvinist teachings of the Rev. Wringhim and, aided and abetted by Gil-Martin, a shadowy figure of evil, he commits a number of crimes, including the murder of his brother George. At the end of the novel, haunted by the diabolic Gil-Martin, he takes his own life.

Gil-Martin is both the living impersonation of the Devil in the folk tradition (and therefore a figure to be feared) and also the agent of evil, the antithesis of Christian virtue, capable of taking possession of Robert's soul and causing him to turn to evil. This dualism between inner and outer reality leads Robert to believe himself to be two people, and the concept of a divided personality is the novel's dominant theme.

That sense of duality within a fictional hero or heroine – the destroyer who both loves and hates the object of obliteration, the sinner who is justified – is a recurring theme in Scottish fiction. Through her use of it in *The Prime of Miss Jean Brodie*, Muriel Spark wrote a novel whose 'Scottishness' can be proved.

In a sense the creation of Miss Jean Brodie and her quaint Edinburgh School exorcised Spark's Scottish childhood in much the same way that *The Girls of Slender Means* helped her to lay aside the ghosts of post-war London. Thereafter her novels (with a few exceptions) became less concerned with time and place and less rooted in identifiable localities. The countryside of *Not to Disturb* is scarcely Switzerland; in *The Hothouse by the East River*, New York is a symbol of wealth and the absence of life, 'home of the vivisectors of the mind'; and the Rome of *The Public Image* is a private city.

The publication of *The Prime of Miss Jean Brodie*, with its several obtrusive Scottish themes, allowed Muriel Spark to be identified as a Scottish writer. In 1970, nine years later, Professor Karl Miller described her position as being 'on any serious estimate the foremost living Scottish novelist, she has yet to be admitted to the Northern pantheon', by which he meant that although she was a Scottish writer in the widest interpretation of that category, narrow parochialism required that she was less of a Scottish writer than some of her contemporaries.

While her Edinburgh novel provided Scottish critics with the opportunity of claiming Mrs Spark as their own, its publication gave her substantial financial success; it was made into a stage play by the American writer Jay Presson Allen, a memorable film with Maggie Smith giving a definitive interpretation of the title role, and, more recently, a television serial.

In Scotland, during the same period, the novel of childhood or youth spent in the industrial west of Scotland enjoyed a literary vogue. In this school of proletarian romanticism the most important novels are Alan Sharp's *A Green Tree in Gedde* (1965), Archie Hinds's *The Dear Green Place* (1966), William McIlvanney's *Remedy is None* (1966) and Gordon Williams's *From Scenes Like These* (1968).

McIlvanney, Sharp and Williams are all identifiably Scottish writers in that their early novels were engaged with the backgrounds from which they sprung. 'For me,' McIlvanney has said, 'self-fulfilment in isolation is meaningless; you are what you are in relation to the society you live in.' But, while a novelist must have that solid picture of the society he writes about, lest his characters become detached or mere cardboard cut-outs, society is ever-changing, the values of one age become the taboos of another, judgements alter, views of the past become distorted, and so on. The writer, too, changes, becomes an exile from his or her past – whether that be the working class of the west of Scotland or the middle-class gentility of Edinburgh – and finds it difficult to reconcile that past with the writing.

This was certainly the case with another Scottish novelist, James Kennaway, whose novel *Household Ghosts* was published in the same year as *The Prime of Miss Jean Brodie*. As a Scot, Kennaway was sentimentally attached to a romantic version of his country's past and its traditions, and he was proud of his childhood connections in Perthshire, but he had no interest in the everyday concerns of contemporary Scotland and its society which he disliked for its 'touchy patriotism and conservatism of an unbelievably fast hue'. It is a common enough paradox for the exile that they should both love and hate the land of their birth.

Nationalism, however, is a poor way of judging a writer and his work. It leads to jingoistic posturing and to the kind of critical parochialism that praises a work simply because it is Scottish, charges that have not escaped Scottish literature over the years. As a result, the concept of Scottishness, as interpreted by the country's literature, has remained in a state of confusion.

On the one hand that lack of critical orderliness leads to the exclusion of writers such as William Drummond of Hawthornden (1585–1649), James Thomson (1700–48) and even John Buchan (1875–1940), either because they chose English as their preferred means of literary communication, or because they wanted to live outside Scotland; on the other it will give grudging acceptance to Scottish writers who live elsewhere, provided that their books touch on things Scottish. Muriel Spark falls into both categories. Half Scottish, half English, yet entirely a writer of Scottish formation, she became a 'constitutional exile' – her phrase – and can never escape the consequences of having spent her formative years in Scotland. Her fiction has been made stronger by that condition, and so too has Scottish literature.

A note on the text

The novel first appeared in *The New Yorker* in October 1961 and was published in hardback by Macmillan, London, in 1961. The Penguin paperback edition (first published in 1965), from which page references have been taken, is still in print.

The Prime of Miss Jean Brodie was dramatised by Jay Presson Allen in 1966 and opened in London with Vanessa Redgrave in the title role. The play was then made into a film in 1969 with Maggie Smith playing the role of Jean Brodie.

Part 2

Summaries
of THE PRIME OF
MISS JEAN BRODIE

A general summary

The novel is briefly told in some 60,000 words and the main characters
and their roles are introduced in the opening pages. The title comes from
the belief of the main character, Miss Jean Brodie, that having reached the
age of thirty-nine she is in the 'prime' of her life and that it is the good
fortune of the chosen few pupils of her 'set' that she can share it with
them.

The members of her 'set' are: Monica Douglas ('famous mostly for
mathematics which she could do in her brain'), Rose Stanley ('famous for
sex'), Eunice Gardner ('spritely gymnastics and glamorous swimming'),
Sandy Stranger ('famous for her vowel sounds'), Jenny Gray ('the prettiest
and most graceful girl of the set'), and Mary Macgregor ('whose fame
rested on her being a silent lump'). The final girl, Joyce Emily Hammond,
only joins the school in the final years although she too is determined to
'get into the famous set'. The girls are also known, with religious inten-
tion, as Miss Brodie's 'disciples'.

From the very beginning of the novel, Miss Brodie emerges as a mass of
apparent contradictions. She tells the girls that she distrusts the Roman
Catholic church yet spends her holidays in Italy and worships Italian
church art. She kicks against the school's team spirit and denounces
middle-class morality but she is a fervent admirer of Mussolini and his
fascists. Forever proclaiming the splendour of passionate love, she settles
for a clandestine affair with the worthy Mr Lowther while refusing the
romantic art teacher Teddy Lloyd because he is a married man.

She is also dogmatic. Giotto is preferred to Leonardo da Vinci as the
greatest Italian artist, simply because she likes his work and not because of
any intrinsic artistic superiority. Mussolini is praised without any understanding of the political changes in Europe at that time – the 1930s. And
the girls are made to agree with their teacher's recommendations, almost
as if they are Miss Brodie's surrogates and not the individuals she would
prefer them to be. As the novel progresses the girls, however, become
aware of the dichotomy of her interests and begin to question them.

It is left to Sandy to be the agent of Miss Brodie's destruction. Gradually
she becomes aware that the girls have been forced to become an élite and
that they are little more than pale images of their teacher's dreams and

aspirations. When Miss Brodie attempts vicariously to satisfy her love for Teddy Lloyd by encouraging Rose Stanley to sleep with him, Sandy takes the initiative and becomes his mistress while Miss Brodie is visiting Hitler's Germany.

As a result Sandy Stranger arranges for Miss Brodie's dismissal by informing the headmistress, the stern Miss Mackay, of Miss Brodie's promotion of fascism – especially in the case of Joyce Emily Hammond whom she has persuaded to go to Spain and fight for Franco in the Spanish Civil War, and who dies there, without ever understanding the issues.

Later in life, Sandy becomes a Roman Catholic and as Sister Helen of the Transfiguration withdraws from the world after writing a 'psychological treatise on the nature of moral perception' called 'The Transformation of the Commonplace'. Significantly, when she is asked what was the main influence on the creation of the book, Sandy replies, 'There was a Miss Jean Brodie in her prime'.

Detailed summaries

NOTE: The novel is divided into six separate chapters of differing length but within each chapter there are several sub-divisions – marked by gaps in the text – which introduce changes of pace or flashbacks and flash-forwards in the narrative.

Chapter 1

The first chapter opens outside the Marcia Blaine School in Edinburgh and quickly establishes the identities of the six girls who make up Miss Brodie's 'set'. It is quite obvious that they are different from the other girls at the school and that they are keen to accentuate those differences. Each one of them is 'famous', or at least well-known within the school for an attribute. Now in the fourth form, they have all known each other since their days in junior school – with the exception of a new girl, Joyce Emily Hammond, who is obviously very keen to join the set.

The presence of the boys on their bicycles reinforces the idea that this is a girl's school with its own rules and values. The Marcia Blaine School caters for middle-class Edinburgh girls. Its prevailing ethos is introduced briefly but effectively: the founder, Marcia Blaine, has a 'manly' portrait below which sits a bunch of 'hard-wearing' flowers and the biblical text reinforces the importance of female virtue.

Miss Jean Brodie is introduced with broad brushstrokes to establish her character. Not only is she an unconventional teacher whose interests range from Italian art to the fascists, but she is willing, even eager, to confide in her pupils. As she leaves the school and passes her group of girls she informs them that there is 'a new plot' to force her to resign from her post.

Having discussed the problem Miss Brodie reminds the girls that any attempt to oust her will fail because she is in the prime of her life.

Her hold on the girls is reinforced by a flashback to six years earlier when she taught them in the junior school. Taking the lesson outside beneath a big elm tree she turns the lesson to her own experience of love and war. She tells them the story of her lost fiancé, Hugh, who was killed during the First World War, one week before the Armistice of November 1918.

The sentimental story of their doomed love is bound in with the story of the Battle of Flodden, one of the great tragedies in Scottish history and it has an emotional effect on the girls. At no point does Miss Brodie attempt to explain the reasons for the First World War or the harsh reality of the fighting on the western front. She is simply playing on their emotions. As Rose Stanley begins to weep, Miss Mackay the headmistress appears and asks what is wrong. The girls show their loyalty to Miss Brodie by agreeing with her explanation that she was giving them a history lesson.

The chapter ends with the hapless and stupid Mary Macgregor getting into trouble for not paying attention. When she is asked what is 'golden', instead of correctly answering 'silence', she listens to Sandy's malicious whisper and answers 'the falling leaves'.

NOTES AND GLOSSARY:

panama hats: broad-brimmed straw hats and part of the girls' school uniform. The ways in which the girls wear their hats is an indication of their different characters and personalities

Buchmanites: followers of the American evangelist Frank Nathan Daniel Buchman (1878–1961) who was the founder of the Oxford Group and its development, Moral Rearmament. Popular in the 1930s, the movement encouraged young people to confess their misdemeanours

Mussolini: Benito Mussolini (1883–1945), Italian fascist dictator who came to power in 1922 and embarked on an ambitious and grandiose programme of expensive public works, and imperial expansion in Africa. Although he was first admired for bringing a measure of stability to Italy, he joined forces with Germany during the Second World War, and was subsequently executed

witch-hazel: an astringent of the leaves and bark of the plant of the same name

'menarche': the onset of first menstruation

Winnie the Pooh: popular children's novel by A. A. Milne (1882–

1956), published in 1926 and featuring a bear of little brain of the same name

Charlotte Brontë: English novelist (1816–85) and author of *Jane Eyre* (1847). Jane Eyre was the first physically plain heroine in the English novel. With its romantic plot it enjoyed an instant success

Einstein: Albert Einstein. One of the best known scientists of his day (1879–1955) who created the Theory of Relativity. He was awarded the Nobel Prize for Physics in 1921

Battle of Flodden: a crucial battle fought between the armies of Scotland and England on 9 September 1517 which resulted in the deaths of King James IV of Scotland together with several Scottish nobles and members of the Royal household

Garibaldi: Giuseppe Garibaldi (1807–82). Italian patriot and politician who played a major role in uniting the small principalities of Italy into one country

lectern: a reading desk, usually in a church, but in this case in the school hall

'O where shall I find a virtuous woman, for her price is above rubies': biblical quotation from the Book of Proverbs, 31:10. This has been misquoted from the original in the King James Bible: 'Who can find a virtuous woman? for her price is far above rubies'

'She left the web ... look'd down to Camelot': lines from the poem 'The Lady of Shalott' by Alfred, Lord Tennyson (1808–92)

Pentland Hills: a range of hills to the south of Edinburgh which form a dramatic visual backdrop to the city

crème de la crème: (*French*) the cream of the cream; the ultimate, the best people, used in this instance by Jean Brodie to describe her pupils

'Give me a girl at an impressionable age, and she is mine for life': an echo of the injunction that a boy introduced to the Jesuit religious order in childhood will remain in it for ever

Stanley Baldwin: Conservative British prime minister in 1923–24, 1924–29 and 1935–37. His motto, 'Safety first', typified his middle-of-the-road, middle-class view of government

Biarritz: a fashionable resort in south-west France on the Atlantic coast

Leonardo da Vinci: Florentine artist (1452–1519) who painted, amongst other masterpieces, the 'Mona Lisa'. He was also a scientific innovator who created notes and diagrams for ambitious engineering schemes

Giotto: Italian painter (1266–1337) who paved the way for the freedom of expression found in Renaissance art. Amongst his finest creations are the altar-piece in the Uffizi and the frescoes in Santa Croce, both in Florence

Joan of Arc: St Jeanne d'Arc (*c.* 1412–31) French heroine who was the inspiration behind King Charles VII's attempts to defeat the English at Orléans in 1429. She was later found guilty of heresy and witchcraft and burned at the stake

'Season of mists and mellow fruitfulness': the opening lines of John Keats's poem 'To Autumn'

Armistice: the end of the First World War on 11 November 1918. It was commemorated with the observance of two minutes' silence at 11 a.m.

the Kaiser: Kaiser (emperor) Wilhelm II of Germany during the First World War and regarded as a 'hate' figure by sections of the British public

Flowers of the Forest: a song composed by Jean Elliot of Minto to commemorate the Scots killed at the Battle of Flodden in 1517. Its words and tune have taken on the attributes of a national air of lament

---

Chapter 2

A flashforward shows that Mary Macgregor has always been the outsider in the group, the girl who was never privy to all of Miss Brodie's secrets. During the Second World War, while serving in the Women's Royal Naval Service she dies in a hotel fire in Cumberland, still ignorant of all that has happened before in her life. The moment of the flashforward occurs when Mary is accused of spilling ink on the classroom floor.

At this stage in their lives, at the age of ten, the girls are told by Miss Brodie that the best is still to come, that they are going to be 'the crème de la crème'. Sandy and Jenny ponder their futures and consider the matter of sex. Jenny tells Sandy that sexual intercourse happens on the 'spur of the moment' – her information comes from the experience of one of her father's female employees who has become pregnant. The realistic Sandy responds that, surely, the urge would have passed by the time they had removed their clothes.

During a birthday tea party at Sandy's house they set to work on 'The Mountain Eyrie', an imaginary story about Miss Brodie's dead lover Hugh

Carruthers. In their version Hugh has not been killed in the war but returns to find that Miss Brodie 'loved another'. Throughout the novel the girls, Sandy and Jenny in particular, are fascinated by Miss Brodie's sexual relationships.

Sandy's imagination also comes to the fore in Miss Brodie's classes, especially when she is reading poetry – an activity that allows her to pretend to converse with characters such as the Lady of Shalott. While the poem is being read Sandy imagines herself asking the Lady of Shalott how her name came to be written on the prow of the boat which took her to Shalott. Or, during a walk, she is able to summon up Alan Breck Stewart, the romantic hero of Robert Louis Stevenson's novel, *Kidnapped*. This introduces the reader to the fact that Sandy has her own double life to stave off boredom.

The chapter introduces Mr Lowther, the school's singing teacher who is Miss Brodie's lover – although at this stage the information remains unrevealed. To the girls she says that they alone are her vocation and that she would refuse any offer of marriage even if it came from the Lord Lyon King-of-Arms, Scotland's principal heraldic officer.

There is also Miss Lockhart, the vivacious science teacher who gives the girls a glimpse beyond the world of Miss Brodie's interest in the liberal arts. When her pupils show signs of being fascinated by science, Miss Brodie reminds them that art is greater than science.

By the end of 1931, their first year with Miss Brodie, the girls in her set have been chosen and, in turn, she rewards them with confidential information about her position in the school and the threats she faces from the headmistress. In a flashforward to later life Eunice, now married to a doctor, tells her husband about Miss Brodie. When they next visit Edinburgh, she says, she wants to put flowers on her grave. She makes it clear that Miss Brodie had a strong effect on her upbringing.

During a walk with Miss Brodie the girls are taken from the middle-class New Town into the area of the Old Town, the old medieval quarter of Edinburgh which was in a state of advanced decay and poverty in the 1930s. Once again Sandy shows a malicious side to her nature when she refuses to take Mary Macgregor's hand and retreats into her world of make-believe with Alan Breck Stewart.

When they see a group of unemployed men, Miss Brodie makes the absurd contention that the problem has been solved in Italy. For Sandy, brought up in a polite suburb, it is like entering a foreign country and she and the other girls look at the poor as if they are strangers. In a flash-forward to the time when she has become a nun and famous theological author, Sandy is visited by a male scholar who was also educated in Edinburgh. As a boy he was delighted by the city's varied architecture, but Sandy can only remember the slums in the Canongate. For both of them Edinburgh was two different cities.

Like the divided city, Miss Brodie is also full of contradictions. Some become apparent during the walk – she abhors the team spirit of the Girl Guides, for instance, but keeps her girls well disciplined. For Sandy this provides a flash of insight: 'the Brodie set was Miss Brodie's fascisti'.

Towards the end of the walk Miss Brodie tells the girls that she is in disagreement with the headmistress about her methods of instruction but that she is determined to stick to them. As with most of Miss Brodie's discourses she expects full agreement from her girls. Once again Sandy retreats into her world of make-believe and when Miss Brodie invites the girls to come to her flat she refuses, pleading that she has a cold. The sight of the unemployed in the poverty-stricken Old Town and the slow revelation of her feelings about Miss Brodie have thoroughly unsettled her – although as soon as she gets home she regrets the decision.

NOTES AND GLOSSARY:

Wrens:	the Women's Royal Naval Service, taken from its initials WRNS
Cumberland:	county in north-west England, now part of Cumbria
Puddocky:	an area in Edinburgh beside the Water of Leith. 'Puddock' is the Scots word for 'frog'
Duchess of York:	Lady Elizabeth Bowes-Lyon, wife of Prince Albert, the Duke of York who became King George VI in 1936, following the abdication of his brother King Edward VIII
musquash:	the fur of the musk-rat, used in the manufacture of coats for women
festal:	festive, joyous
Mountain Eyrie:	literally the nest of an eagle in a remote mountain area but here used poetically to describe the hiding place of Miss Brodie's lover Hugh Carruthers in the story written by Sandy and Jenny
lithe:	pliant, supple, athletic
azure:	clear blue
Hallowe'en:	the festival of All Hallows Day, celebrated on 31 October
thingummyjig:	slang for a thing, or person, of which the speaker cannot or will not remember its name, in this instance a penis
Dean Bridge:	a bridge over the Water of Leith in Edinburgh designed by Thomas Telford in 1831
gym tunic:	one-piece dress worn by girls as part of their school uniform
***The Lady of Shalott*:**	poem by Alfred, Lord Tennyson (1808–92)

Mona Lisa: portrait of the wife of Francesco del Giocondo by Leonardo da Vinci, famous for its enigmatic smile. It hangs in the Louvre in Paris

'The babe leapt in her womb': from The Gospel According to St Luke, 1:41, foretelling the birth of Jesus Christ

Lord Lyon King-of-Arms: the chief officer of arms of Scotland

Sybil Thorndike: English actress (1882–1976) who was best known in the 1930s for her role of Joan of Arc in Bernard Shaw's play *St Joan*

box-pleat tweeds: a pleated tweed skirt

endowed rates: reduced fees permitted by the money left by the founder of the school

Ariel: a spirit in William Shakespeare's play *The Tempest* who assists Prospero in the pursuit of his magic schemes

the Festival: the Edinburgh International Festival, founded in 1947, takes place each year for three weeks in August and September

Meccanos: Meccano sets, boy's toy construction sets based on engineering principles

***Kidnapped*:** novel by Robert Louis Stevenson published in 1886. It is set against the Jacobite rebellion of 1745 and one of the main characters is the adventurous romantic Jacobite Alan Breck Stewart who acts as a foil to the staid Lowlander, David Balfour

Meadows: an open area on the south side of Edinburgh, originally the drained ground of the Burgh Loch

Old Town: the original town of Edinburgh set on the ridge between the Castle Rock and the Palace of Holyroodhouse. Until its regeneration in the 1960s it possessed a large number of ancient and poverty-stricken slum buildings

League of Nations: an international organisation established after the First World War to maintain world order

fascisti: followers of the Italian leader Benito Mussolini. They took their names from the Latin *fasces*, the bound rods and arrows which were the symbol of authority in ancient Rome

Royal Mile: the name given to the Edinburgh street which runs from the Castle to Holyroodhouse. It comprises the Lawnmarket, the High Street, the Canongate and the Abbey Strand

Mary, Queen of Scots: queen of Scotland between 1548 and 1567. One of the great romantic figures in Scottish history, she was executed in 1587 after being implicated in a plot against her cousin Queen Elizabeth of England

Grassmarket: open market area on the south side of the old town of Edinburgh below the Castle

John Knox: Scottish Presbyterian reformer (*c.* 1513–70) who opposed the reign of Mary Queen of Scots. Usually portrayed as a grim and forbidding figure, he was an authoritative preacher and the author of a number of important religious books

Auden: W[ystan] H[ugh] Auden (1907–73), English poet who was one of the best known and most innovative writers of his generation

Eliot: T[homas] S[tearns] Eliot (1888–1965), English poet and dramatist and one of the founders of the modern movement in poetry. His long poem *The Waste Land* (1922) established him as the voice of a generation disillusioned by the First World War. It is revealing that although Miss Brodie considered herself to be an innovator she did not teach her set anything about the poetry of Auden or Eliot

Spanish Civil War: the bitter conflict fought between Spain's republican government and nationalist insurgents, 1936–39, which represented a wider struggle between communism and fascism. Many left-wing volunteers from Britain served in the 'International Brigades' on the side of the republicans. As an admirer of Mussolini and Hitler, Miss Brodie supports General Franco's nationalists – a curious choice for a self-confessed educational reformer

Calvinism: the system of theology evolved by the French Protestant reformer John Calvin (1509–64) which forms the basis of the presbyterian Church of Scotland. In its more extreme form, it has led to the 'elect' who believe that all their actions are justified, whether morally right or wrong

St Giles: the High Kirk (church) of St Giles, founded in the twelfth century and situated in the Royal Mile and Edinburgh's main presbyterian church

Prodigal Son: parable from the Gospel according to St Luke, 16: 11–32 in which a wasteful younger son squanders his inheritance but is still welcomed back into his father's household

Presbyterian: a form of Protestant theology and doctrine which forms the basis and government of the Church of

	Scotland. Like Calvinism it is generally held to be a rigorously puritanical and joyless form of religion
Episcopalian:	literally rule by bishops, but in Scotland, applied to the Scottish Episcopal Church
John Buchan:	novelist and statesman and the author of *The Thirty Nine Steps*
James Hogg:	(1770–1835) poet and novelist, also known as 'The Ettrick Shepherd'. His long poem 'Kilmeny' tells the story of a young virgin, Kilmeny, who is removed for seven years to a faery or spirit world. It is taken from *The Queen's Wake* (1813)
Churchhill:	middle-class suburb in south Edinburgh
hacking laughs:	raucous, coughing laughter

Chapter 3

The chapter opens in 1931, the last year which Miss Brodie's set will spend with her in the junior school. The narrator reminds the reader that Miss Brodie was not alone in feeling that she was a spinster in her prime. Many other women in Edinburgh enjoyed the same intellectual curiosity about modern life: the loss of so many young men during the First World War was one of the reasons why they remained unmarried.

At the beginning of their opening lesson Miss Brodie tells them about her summer holiday in Italy and of her admiration for Mussolini and his fascist followers. She also reminds them that she is in her prime – this device is used throughout the novel to reinforce Miss Brodie's personality. However, Miss Mackay returns the girls to reality by reminding them that they must study hard for their qualifying examination for the senior school.

It is also clear that Miss Brodie's behaviour has roused the antagonism of her colleagues – with the exception of Gordon Lowther, the singing master, and Teddy Lloyd, the married art teacher, who both compete for her attention. During an art appreciation lesson the girls are overcome with giggles by Lloyd's treatment of the curves of the female figure in Botticelli's *Primavera*.

Their sexual awakening is increased by speculation over Miss Brodie's relationship with both men and over the vexed question of whether or not Monica Douglas saw Mr Lloyd kissing Miss Brodie. In a flashforward, Miss Brodie tells Sandy that she was indeed in love with Teddy Lloyd but renounced him because he was a married man and a Catholic.

During Miss Brodie's and Mr Lowther's absence from school – an incident which causes much comment amongst the staff – Sandy and Jenny speculate about the possibility of a sexual relationship between the two teachers. Even the sight of the sewing-machine's shuttle going 'up and down' has sexual connotations and the girls engage in much heated consideration about their teacher's sexual life. While Miss Brodie is absent they are taught by Miss Gaunt, an elderly spinster who makes them work hard. There is a striking contrast between her and Miss Brodie's methods: whereas Miss Brodie enjoys reading poetry to her pupils, Miss Gaunt punishes Rose by making her write out a hundred lines from Scott's poem, *Marmion*. Once again, Sandy takes refuge in her fantasy life, this time pretending that she is in conversation with Mr Rochester from Charlotte Brontë's novel, *Jane Eyre*.

As this is the last year before the girls proceed to the secondary school they are interviewed individually by Miss Mackay, the headmistress. Ostensibly this is to enable them to discuss which subjects they will study, but Miss Mackay uses the opportunity to question them about Miss Brodie's teaching methods of which she obviously disapproves. An instance is the visit to the theatre to see Pavlova dancing *Swan Lake*. Miss Brodie tells her girls that they must grow up to be dedicated women, just as she has dedicated herself to them.

When Miss Brodie tells the girls that Pavlova insisted on the highest standards, whatever the cost, Sandy imagines a conversation with the great ballerina. During the course of this, Pavlova sounds like Miss Brodie and this leads to an important flashforward. In later life, when she is dying in a nursing home, Miss Brodie wonders if it was Sandy who betrayed her. Instead of the dedication demanded by Pavlova, and by Miss Brodie, Sandy chooses to become a nun, which, Miss Brodie says, is 'not the sort of dedication I meant'.

The girls' interests are temporarily dampened when a man exposes himself to Jenny but this incident also allows Sandy to extend her make-believe world to include an imagined friendship with the police-woman who investigates the incident. In her fantasies she and the policewoman – Sergeant Ann Grey – work together 'to eliminate sex from Edinburgh and environs' (p. 68). The investigation will also include Miss Brodie's relationships.

The culmination of Sandy's and Jenny's fascination with sex is the concoction of a hilarious romantic fiction which envisages Jean Brodie and Gordon Lowther having sexual intercourse on Arthur's Seat 'while the storm raged about us' (p. 73). On one level this is the continuation of Sandy's and Jenny's fantasies about Miss Brodie, but on another level the story is also the 'evidence' about her sexual impropriety which Sandy wants to give to her fictional policewoman. This is a hint of her future act of betrayal.

NOTES AND GLOSSARY:

Oxford Group: see Buchmanites (Chapter 1)

Scottish Nationalist Movement: campaign for Scottish independence which came into being in 1928 with the formation of the National Party of Scotland. In 1934 the party merged with others to form the Scottish National Party and it won its first parliamentary seat in 1945

Hume: David Hume (1711–76), Scottish empirical philosopher and historian and one of the great thinkers of the eighteenth-century Enlightenment. His *Treatise on Human Nature* (1739–40) argues that all thought is based on experience and not on innate ideas

Boswell: James Boswell (1745–95), Scottish writer and advocate, best known for his biography of the English writer Dr Samuel Johnson

Professor Tovey's Sunday concerts: musical concerts mounted by Professor Donald Tovey, professor of music at the University of Edinburgh

Cimabue: Florentine painter and teacher (*c.* 1240–1302), best known for his panel paintings in Pisa, Florence and Assisi. Giotto was one of his more famous pupils

lace mantilla: a large lace shawl worn by Spanish women over their head and shoulders

Botticelli's *Primavera* which means the Birth of Spring: *Primavera*, literally meaning 'Spring', is an allegorical painting of Venus bedecked with flowers in a joyful celebration of Spring, by the Florentine painter, Sandro Botticelli (*c.* 1445–1510). Miss Brodie displays her woolly-mindedness here by confusing two paintings: *Spring* and *The Birth of Venus*

Ramsay MacDonald: (1866–1917) the first British Labour prime minister who formed a national government with Liberals and Conservatives in 1931

qualifying examination: examination taken at the age of eleven to test the girls before they enter senior school

Dante meeting Beatrice: the celebration of the love of Dante Alighieri (1265–1321) for Beatrice as expressed in the poems of his *Vita Nuova*

Rossetti: Dante Gabriel Rossetti (1828–82), English painter and poet associated with the Pre-Raphaelite movement

Swinburne: Algernon Charles Swinburne (1837–1909), English poet and dramatist, associated with the Pre-Raphaelite movement; his writing was considered to be lacking in morals, and somewhat risqué

'Come autumn sae pensive ... o' nature's decay': lines from the song 'My Nanie's Awa'' by Robert Burns

leaven in the lump: literally the substance added to dough to produce fermentation but in this instance used by Miss Brodie to describe Sandy's superiority to the rest of the 'set'

Marmion: long heroic poem written by Sir Walter Scott in 1808 and sub-titled 'A Tale of Flodden Field'

trepidation: fear, alarm

Cramond: seaside village on the Forth estuary to the west of Edinburgh

Pavlova: Anna Pavlova (1882–1931), Russian ballerina who formed her own touring company and was famous for her solo performances, most notably of the dying swan in the ballet *Swan Lake*

Corstorphine: middle-class suburb in western Edinburgh

a man joyfully exposing himself: a man openly displaying his sexual organs in public

Water of Leith: small river which runs through Edinburgh

plaintiff: the party who brings a suit to a court of law. In Scottish law it is generally known as the 'pursuer'

the Change: the beginning of menstruation

bicker: literally, to attack with sticks or stones; to argue or quarrel

Arthur's Seat: craggy hill of volcanic origin and principal landmark in Edinburgh

bracken: coarse moorland fern

fain: willingly, gladly

'Hey, Johnnie Cope': popular Jacobite song created in celebration of the defeat of the government army under General Sir John Cope at Prestonpans in 1745 by a Jacobite army under Prince Charles Edward Stewart, or 'Bonnie Prince Charlie'

Chapter 4

The girls are now in senior school and coming to terms with a wider range of interesting subjects, such as chemistry which is taught by Miss Lockhart. However, despite being divided into different houses and classes – this is part of Miss Mackay's plans to break them up – the 'Brodie set' refuse to embrace the all-pervasive team spirit thereby earning the displeasure of the headmistress.

In an incident which points to a future occurrence Mary Macgregor panics during a chemistry lesson involving an experiment with magnesium flares – a premonition of her future death in a hotel fire in Cumberland. This prompts two related flashforwards in which both Sandy and Miss Brodie regret their unkind behaviour towards Mary.

During this intense period of induction to the wider range of subjects in the senior school, Miss Brodie keeps in touch with her girls and attempts, vicariously, to share their new enthusiasms, even to the extent of learning Greek with them after school hours. She also reveals to them the extent of her relationship with Gordon Lowther and the attempts made by the school to put a stop to it. Miss Gaunt has encouraged the school's sewing mistresses, the sisters Miss Alison Kerr and Miss Ellen Kerr, to work as his housekeepers. The discovery of Miss Brodie's nightdress in his bed is reported to Miss Gaunt and used as evidence to sack Miss Brodie but Miss Mackay feels that it is insufficient evidence to warrant further action.

Undeterred by the school's disapproval, Miss Brodie spends more time with Lowther at his house in Cramond. The girls are also invited, but in their company Miss Brodie demands to know more about Teddy Lloyd. Not only has he started painting Rose Stanley's portrait but he is anxious to spend time with them because they are members of Miss Brodie's set. At this stage they are thirteen years old.

During the summer holidays Miss Brodie visits Nazi Germany which she imagines to be more 'reliable' than Mussolini's Italy.

NOTES AND GLOSSARY:

'These are bunsen burners ... a retort, a crucible': items of scientific equipment in the school's laboratory

predestination: the religious belief in the divine fore-ordaining of all that will happen, and, more specifically, that sins committed by the elected few cannot imperil their hopes of salvation

hieroglyphics: a type of writing consisting of figures of objects used by the ancient Egyptians. Here used ironically to describe Greek characters

houses: a sub-division of a school to which pupils belong and which is supposed to create team spirit. Originally they were boarding-houses in a private school

graves of the martyrs: the graves of puritanical religious fundamentalists, or Covenanters, killed by government forces after King Charles II attempted to introduce episcopalianism in Scotland

Florence Nightingale: English nurse (1820–1910) who revolutionised the care of wounded soldiers during the Crimean War by introducing new standards of nursing

Cleopatra: Queen of Egypt (c. 69–30BC) whose relationship with the Roman Mark Antony is the subject of Shakespeare's play *Antony and Cleopatra*

Helen of Troy: according to Greek legend, the beautiful daughter of Zeus and Leda. After marrying Menelaus, King of

Sparta, she was seduced by Paris and carried off to Troy, an action which led to the Trojan war

ellipse: a curve in which the points are at an equal distance

John Stuart Mill: English philosopher (1806–73) who advocated 'utilitarianism', a belief that happiness was not an end in itself but should be sought by the pursuit of an altruistic or artistic ideal

c.g. of his load: centre of gravity of his load

Samuel Pepys: English government servant who is best known for his diaries which relate the gossip and scandals of the reign of King Charles II

Church of Rome: the Roman Catholic church

I am a descendant, do not forget, of Willie Brodie: Jean Brodie is proud of the fact that one of her ancestors was William Brodie, a respected eighteenth-century Edinburgh town councillor who led a double life as leader of a gang of burglars and house breakers

Norma Shearer: American film actress (1901–83) who won an Oscar in 1930 for her performance in *The Divorcee*

Elizabeth Bergner: Austrian film and stage actress (1900–86) who was particularly associated with the work of Frank Wedekind (1864–1918). She made her début on the London stage in 1933 as Gemma Jones in *Escape me Never*

It was a large gabled house with a folly-turret: Gordon Lowther's substantial house in Cramond which has a gable-end and a mock Romantic turret

crêpe de Chine: a clinging fabric made of raw silk

Hitler: Adolf Hitler (1889–1945), dictator of Nazi Germany who came to power in 1934. He turned Germany into a one-party state and ruled through a reign of terror which included the widespread and systematic massacre of the Jewish people

Thomas Carlyle: Scottish historian and visionary (1795–1881) who advocated the government of society by strong and just leaders

sweetbreads: the pancreas of an animal cooked as a delicacy

Chapter 5

When Sandy sees Teddy Lloyd's portrait of Rose Stanley she immediately notices that it has the likeness of Jean Brodie. Other portraits of the girls also resemble her. By this time Sandy has become friendly with Teddy and his wife Deirdre but while visiting the studio Sandy is kissed by him.

As the girls grow older Miss Brodie confides in Sandy while they are playing golf together. She says that she has placed all her hopes in her and Rose but there is a sub-text to her comments which becomes apparent later in the novel. She hopes that Rose will become Teddy Lloyd's lover and that Sandy will keep her informed about the affair.

Her vicarious pleasure in this possibility has also been created by the gradual demise of her relationship with Gordon Lowther and the termination of the girls' visits to Cramond. At the end of term he announces his engagement to Miss Lockhart.

Increasingly, during this period, Sandy begins to make connections between Jean Brodie's élite 'set' and the elect of Calvinism as she sees it portrayed in Edinburgh's history and society. The feeling is made more intense when she stands outside the High Church of St Giles with its 'emblems of a dark and terrible salvation' (p. 108). Nevertheless Sandy is tempted to enter the spirit of Miss Brodie's plan and for over a year she agrees to remain an informant and fellow-plotter in her teacher's plans.

When Gordon Lowther marries Miss Lockhart, Miss Brodie puts all her energies into planning a relationship between Teddy Lloyd and Rose.

NOTES AND GLOSSARY:

harlequin outfit: a diamond-patterned costume worn by a pantomime character

The Lloyds were Catholics ... by force: a reference to the fact that Roman Catholics are forbidden to use artificial methods of contraception

fag: slang for cigarette

Silver Jubilee: the celebrations for the twenty-fifth anniversary of the reign of King George V in 1935

dragoman: an interpreter or guide in a country where Arabic, Turkish or Persian is spoken

Fabian Society: the principal intellectual grouping within the Labour Party which seeks to achieve socialism by constitutional, non-revolutionary means

Morningside and Merchiston: middle-class suburbs of south Edinburgh

There was a whiff of sulphur about the idea: in popular belief sulphur, an evil-smelling substance found in volcanic regions, has been associated with the fires of hell. The idea that Sandy should report on Rose's relationship with Teddy Lloyd is seen as being suitably wicked

D. H. Lawrence: D[avid] H[erbert] Lawrence (1885–1930), novelist who created strong-willed heroines in novels such as *Sons and Lovers* (1913) and *Lady Chatterley's Lover* (1928). Much of his work is concerned with sexual freedom and frankness

personal calumny: a slander or false accusation against an individual
The Scotsman: daily newspaper published in Edinburgh

Chapter 6

When the girls are seventeen they find that Miss Mackay is still interested in getting evidence that can lead to Miss Brodie's being sacked. Despite frequent questioning, the girls remain loyal, although all are developing separate and different interests. A new member joins the set: Joyce Emily Hammond, a wealthy girl with a disturbed past. She, too, is taken up by Miss Brodie, but her life is cut short when she runs away to join her brother in the Spanish Civil War and is killed when her train is bombed.

In the summer of 1938 after the last of the Brodie set leaves school Sandy has a love affair with Teddy Lloyd but is disconcerted to discover that all his portraits of the girls and his family still resemble Miss Brodie. When her old teacher discovers the affair, she is at first upset that her plans have gone awry but is then pleased that she still has a surrogate in his bed.

After leaving school Sandy studies psychology but continues to meet Miss Brodie. During one meeting in the autumn of 1938 she learns that Miss Brodie encouraged Joyce Emily Hammond to go to Spain to fight on Franco's side – even though her brother was serving on the opposition communist side. This information encourages Sandy to give evidence to Miss Mackay of Jean Brodie's interests in fascism. At the end of the school year in 1939 Jean Brodie is obliged to leave the school. At the time Britain was preparing to go to war against Nazi Germany and her political leanings provide the headmistress with an apposite excuse to dismiss her.

Sandy excuses the betrayal by claiming that Miss Brodie had betrayed her set by living her life through them – playing God with them, as she sees it. Although Miss Brodie could have been sacked for sexual impropriety, Sandy chooses politics as the most practical means. In a flashforward Miss Brodie writes to Sandy about her dismissal and informs her that politics were only an excuse: the headmistress had tried to find evidence of 'immorality' on several occasions but had always failed. The letter ends with the disturbing information – to Miss Brodie at least – that it was one of her girls who had 'betrayed' her. Although Miss Brodie suspects that it might have been Monica she excuses Sandy from any guilt.

In further flashforwards each of the remaining members of the set visits Sandy, now a nun in her convent. Jenny tells her about falling in love with a man in Rome and wishing that she could have told Miss Brodie. Eunice tells her about putting flowers on Miss Brodie's grave, but it is left to Monica to tell her that before Miss Brodie died she suspected that Sandy had betrayed her. Sandy replies that betrayal is only possible when loyalty is deserved.

Later Sandy becomes a nun, thereby following Teddy Lloyd's religion, but she is still uncertain about the moral rectitude of her act of betrayal. The novel ends with Sandy, now Sister Helena of the Transfiguration, desperately clutching the bars of her cell and admitting to a visitor that the major influence of her schooldays was in fact Miss Brodie.

NOTES AND GLOSSARY:

Miss Mackay, the headmistress ... the Brodie set: the headmistress never stopped asking them questions about Miss Brodie – in order to discover evidence which would incriminate her

matriarchally: in the manner of a woman ruler

switch of hair: a long bunch or coil of hair

carnality: sensuality

renunciation: the act of giving up or disowning. Miss Brodie deliberately uses religious terminology to describe the ending of her relationship with Teddy Lloyd

Fay Compton: English actress (1894–1978) who began her career as a music-hall artiste but later graduated to stage, film and television. During the 1920s and 1930s she was particularly well known for her interpretation of Shakespearean roles

Part 3

Commentary

Narrative structure

The opening passage of the novel poses a rhetorical question taken from the Book of Proverbs (31:10) – 'Who can find a virtuous woman? for her price is far above rubies.' The rest of the novel is an attempt to answer the question as it is applied to Miss Jean Brodie and, to a lesser extent, to her girls.

Although there is a strong narrative line which chronicles the emergence of Miss Brodie's 'prime', the novel has a complicated system of flashbacks and flashforwards in time. It opens in 1936, when the girls are in secondary school, returns to 1930, the year of the beginning of Miss Brodie's prime, and ends in 1939 when she is dismissed from school for teaching fascism. However, it also ranges forward to the girls' adult years and to 1946 when Miss Brodie is reported to have died of cancer. Although she hoped that her prime would last until she was sixty, the reader is told that she died at the age of fifty-six.

The a-chronological narrative allows the reader to understand Miss Brodie's hold over her girls by foretelling the consequences of her actions. Mary Macgregor, who is virtually ignored and scorned, dies alone in a hotel fire; pretty Jenny Gray becomes an actress; sensible Monica Douglas marries a scientist; Eunice Gardiner becomes a nurse married to a doctor; Rose Stanley, 'famous for sex', marries a businessman; and Sandy Stranger, the betrayer of Miss Brodie, becomes a nun in a church where she finds 'quite a number of Fascists much less agreeable than Miss Brodie' (p. 125).

Spark's narrative technique is also important for creating the characters. For example, Mary Macgregor's death in a hotel fire is foreseen when she panics during an experiment with magnesium flares during a chemistry lesson. Similarly, Monica Douglas's bad temper as a girl remains with her throughout her life: when she visits Sandy in later life she is facing a breakdown in her marriage after attacking her sister-in-law. Jenny forgets the moment of sexual awakening until she is in her forties when she meets a man in Rome and is touched again 'by a reawakening of that same buoyant and airy discovery of sex' (p. 80).

The flashback is an acknowledged literary method which allows the novelist to clarify or explain the main action or development of the main characters. By glancing back into the past it is possible to understand the present more completely. For example, although the novel opens at a time when the girls are in secondary school, the flashbacks to an earlier period explain and underscore the hold which Miss Brodie has over them. These flashbacks are introduced unobtrusively and without explanation and it is one of the strengths of Spark's narrative structure that past, present and future can exist as one.

Similarly, although less frequently used in fiction, the use of flash-forwards is also a device for a clearer understanding of the main characters. It explains their motives and provides a deeper insight into the development of their personalities, especially Sandy's and Miss Brodie's. In this novel, too, the flashforward reinforces the sense of predestination: just as Miss Brodie believes in the principle of an 'elect' whose actions are preordained, so, too, is the reader allowed to see the consequences of their actions.

In fact, Miss Brodie is a constant and commanding presence who projects her moral rectitude throughout the school, ignoring her colleagues and 'flattening their scorn beneath the chariot wheels of her superiority, and deviating her head towards them no more than an insulting half-inch' (p. 54). Although only barely mentioned in the novel, her own death is the stuff of poetic tragedy: 'Her name and her memory, after her death, flitted from mouth to mouth like swallows in summer, and in winter they were gone' (p. 127). She is also discussed as if she were a real person living in a real setting: at the beginning of Chapter 3 Spark writes about Jean Brodie in matter-of-fact tones which suggests that she has a separate and identifiable existence. The novel's title makes it clear, too, that Jean Brodie is the main character around which all the action develops.

Themes

The themes of any novel are the ideas presented by an author within the narrative. They are also developed by the characters who might comment upon them or, through their actions, add to the reader's understanding of what the novelist is attempting to convey. In *The Prime of Miss Jean Brodie* there are several related themes but the dominant idea within the novel is the examination of betrayal. It is around this theme that the novel is constructed.

Betrayal

The betrayal of one human by another is considered to be one of the worst crimes of commission, that is, one which is deliberately and knowingly done. It is also central to the Christian faith: Jesus's disciple Peter betrays him three times after he is arrested and taken before Caiaphas, the high priest. This Jesus has foreseen but it does not present Peter from denying that he knew him: 'And Peter remembered the word of Jesus, which said unto him, Before the cock crow, thou shalt deny me thrice. And he went out and wept bitterly' (Matthew 26:75). Given Spark's use of biblical language and imagery throughout the novel – the girls are regarded as Miss Brodie's 'disciples' and she talks about 'renouncing' her lovers in favour of her set – the betrayal of Miss Brodie has an obvious Christian connotation.

The theme of betrayal in this novel, though, is centred on the figure of Sandy Stranger who chooses to break faith with Miss Brodie in three different but connected ways. First, she becomes Teddy Lloyd's lover, thereby taking Miss Brodie's place in his bed and thwarting the ambition that it should be Rose. Having done so, this leads to the discovery that he can only reproduce the likeness of Jean Brodie in all his portraits of the 'set'. While caught up in the position of sex-surrogate and go-between, Sandy attempts to discover why Lloyd is fascinated by such a 'ridiculous' woman, and also to understand Miss Brodie's fear of committing herself to a married Catholic man. As her pre-occupation with the problem runs its course she stumbles on politics as the means of destruction – it is 1939 and Miss Brodie is still fascinated by the fascists. 'I am not really interested in world affairs,' Sandy tells the headmistress, 'only in stopping Miss Brodie'. This is clearly a case of the end justifying the means.

Secondly, although Sandy's decision to betray her teacher is based on politics, her underlying argument is prompted by Miss Brodie's corruption of morality. ('You won't be able to pin her down on sex,' she lies to Miss Mackay, in the knowledge that not only has Miss Brodie been sleeping with Gordon Lowther but she has also schemed to get one of her girls into bed with Teddy Lloyd.) Sandy also destroys Miss Brodie because she understands that she believes too firmly in the doctrine of Calvinism, the conviction that she and her set are of the elect who can do as they please and that the rest of the school are of the Damned: 'She thinks she is Providence, thought Sandy, she thinks she is the god of Calvin, she sees the beginning and the end' (p. 120). This is the ultimate heresy for the Catholicism which Sandy is later to adopt.

Finally, by becoming a Catholic and then a nun, Sandy breaks faith with her teacher's lifelong distaste for the Roman Catholic religion. This metamorphosis can also be regarded as an act of betrayal even though Miss Brodie refuses to regard it as such: in her simple-minded way, she merely wonders if it was done to 'annoy' her.

And yet, there is more than a hint of hypocrisy in Sandy's actions. When Miss Brodie asks her for the identity of the girl who betrayed her she excuses herself by claiming that the word betrayal does not apply: 'If you did not betray us it is impossible that you could have been betrayed by us' (p. 126). In other words, speaking like 'an enigmatic Pope', Sandy knows that Miss Brodie betrayed the girls because she attempted to manipulate their lives, but she also knows that Miss Brodie can never understand the extent of that betrayal. This is made clear in a flashforward to 1946 when Miss Brodie talks to Sandy about the identity of the girl who betrayed her.

Just as Miss Brodie played God with her set, so too has Sandy set herself up as judge and executioner and the novel ends on an ambiguous note with Sandy, now a nun, unsure about the moral correctness of her betrayal of Miss Brodie. Having ruined her mentor, she has retired from the world – a suitably religious reaction to her behaviour.

The divided personality

Edinburgh, the city of contrasts, provides the background for the contradictions in Jean Brodie's own personality: she is very much a product of her own environment. Sandy Stranger comes to an early understanding of this dichotomy when the Brodie set are taken for a walk through the squalor of the Old Town which is contrasted unfavourably with the wealth and comfort of the Georgian New Town and the outlying suburbs.

It is also a place in which the Calvinism of John Knox has been both built into the architecture and fashioned the thinking of its citizens. Early on, Sandy sees that there is a link between Miss Brodie's espousal of her set as the 'crème de la crème' and the precepts of the predestined elect.

A similar dichotomy is present in Miss Brodie and this leads her to espouse an absurd combination of ideals. She admires Mussolini's fascist Italy yet berates the team spirit fostered by the Girl Guides: 'Perhaps the Guides were too much of a rival fascisti, and Miss Brodie could not bear it' (p. 32). She encourages a sense of individuality amongst the girls she teaches but will not let them speak their minds: she informs them that Giotto is always to be preferred to Leonardo da Vinci for no other reason than the former is her 'favourite'.

She is a lover of things Mediterranean, especially Italian culture, yet she fears the Catholic church, because it caters for people 'who did not want to think for themselves' (p. 85). She denies herself the love of the romantic artist Teddy Lloyd because he is a Catholic and a married man, but sees nothing wrong in sharing the bed of Gordon Lowther, the music master.

Given so many contradictions and a style of teaching that borders on the ideology of the fascists she so admires, Jean Brodie is disliked by her fellow teachers. But as Spark makes clear, Miss Brodie is only set apart from the school by her ideas and is still a respectable lady in her private life (pp. 42–3). She is described as being similar to many other progressive spinsters who lived in Edinburgh in the 1930s, many of whom had lost loved ones during the First World War.

Unable to act out her own philosophy – prevented both by convention and by the passing of her prime – Miss Brodie encourages her group of schoolgirls to become her surrogates. She inspires Joyce Emily to go to

Spain to fight for Franco (where she loses her life). She attempts (but fails) to ease Rose Stanley into Teddy Lloyd's bed. The remaining girls in the Brodie set fulfil other functions but it is Sandy Stranger, who most resembles Miss Brodie, who becomes her mentor's eyes and ears. In effect, she becomes the other half of Miss Brodie: 'Sandy was never bored, but she had to lead a double life of her own in order never to be bored' (p. 21).

And just as Miss Brodie's world is never realistic and based largely on make-believe – significantly none of the crème de la crème reach their own primes – so also does Sandy Stranger manufacture her own form of fantasy. With Jenny Gray she composes 'The Mountain Eyrie', a romantic story about Hugh Carruthers, Jean Brodie's fiancé, who was killed in the First World War. She has imaginary conversations with literary figures such as the Lady of Shalott, Mr Rochester from Charlotte Brontë's *Jane Eye* and Alan Breck, the romantic hero of Robert Louis Stevenson's novel, *Kidnapped*. She also casts herself in the role of one of Pavlova's pupils after Miss Brodie has taken them to the ballet but try as she may it is her teacher who intrudes in the form of the famous ballerina.

Sandy uses the fantasies as a buffer between her and Miss Brodie, and as the novel unfolds, and Sandy matures, so does reality break into her perception of that relationship. It is significant that Sandy always understands the difference between fantasy and reality and that her musings on the former stop after the onset of adolescence. Early in the novel, Spark has provided a clue to Jean Brodie's dual personality and to Sandy's understanding of it. While still in the junior school, Sandy notices that some days Miss Brodie's 'chest was flat, no bulges at all'; on others, though, 'her chest was breast-shaped and large, very noticeable'.

The realisation that Jean Brodie can be two people – radical teacher with the best interests of her pupils at heart, and immoral leader willing to sacrifice them in her own interests – is central to the novel and it is through Sandy Stranger that we perceive it. Having become Miss Brodie's closest confidante and a sounding board for her ambitions, Sandy finds that she has become the one member of the set who can use her authority for good or for evil. She has learned well from her teacher and can now make her or break her.

Calvinism and Catholicism

Muriel Spark converted to Catholicism in 1954 but she was brought up in presbyterian Edinburgh, a city whose history reflects Scotland's traditional links with Calvinist Protestantism. Her father was Jewish and her mother belonged to the Church of England but it is the contrast between the churches of Rome and John Calvin which informs much of her best work, including *The Prime of Miss Jean Brodie*.

From the outset of the novel it is made clear that Miss Brodie does not approve of Catholicism. Although she admits to her girls that she met the Pope during a visit to Rome she gets a small measure of satisfaction by claiming that she did not actually kiss his ring but merely hovered her lips over it. When she mentions Catholicism it is to tell them that the religion only attracts those who do not want to think for themselves. And yet the narrator informs us that Catholicism could have saved her, or at least 'normalised' her.

On one level, the conversion of Sandy Stranger to Catholicism is a fitting culmination of the novel. Although she comes from a family which is described as being 'not church-going' she has to reject Presbyterianism as a creed before she can even think of embracing Catholicism. The moment comes to her when she inspects the relics of Edinburgh's Calvinist heritage and understands the full meaning of the doctrine of the elect, by which a select few are saved while the rest are condemned to outer darkness.

When she makes the connection between the Calvinist elect and Miss Brodie's set, she finds that she is ready to reject both Calvinism and Miss Brodie's methods. By then she has already made the connection between the creation of the set and Miss Brodie's fascination with fascism – significantly, the realisation dawns during a walk through divided Edinburgh – and she can fully comprehend the extent of Miss Brodie's desire to control their lives. More than anything else in the novel, the gulf between teacher and pupil is illuminated by Sandy's rejection of Calvinism and her decision to enter the Catholic Church. This realisation allows her to believe that she has acted virtuously by 'putting a stop to Miss Brodie'.

Nevertheless, although Sandy embraces Catholicism and joins a reclusive order of nuns it is by no means certain that she has found peace of mind in her new religion. Not only does she admit that the Catholic Church contains a number of fascists less agreeable than Miss Brodie but when friends visit her in her cell she is not composed but grips the bars of the grille as if she wants to escape. This is not the picture of a woman at ease with herself.

Fascism

The main action of the novel covers the years of the 1930s when fascism as a political philosophy came to prominence in Mussolini's Italy and Hitler's Germany. Not only does Miss Brodie consider both leaders to be her heroes but she also admires General Franco, the right-wing nationalist leader whose Falangist party seized power in Spain at the end of a long and brutal civil war.

Her fascination with fascism is another example of the dichotomy of her beliefs. She is dismissive of the Girl Guides and discourages her set from taking part in team games at school, yet she admires the black-shirted fascisti who marched behind Mussolini. Her summer-time visits to Italy encourage her to believe that fascism is the way forward and that Mussolini is 'one of the greatest men in the world' (p. 44). Later she comes to believe the same of the Nazi leader of Germany, Adolf Hitler.

On one level her admiration is absurd and simple-minded and is based solely on her own prejudiced beliefs. Many other people of her class and background shared similar beliefs during the 1930s. For example, she makes the ridiculous claim that under Mussolini unemployment will be abolished. On another level, though, her fascination with fascism mirrors her own style of teaching and her own attitude towards life. While claiming that she bases everything on the need to lead out, from the Latin verb *educare*, she is hopelessly dogmatic. Her opinions and beliefs are forced upon her set, whose members are not allowed to have their own opinions and are resented when they express them. In that sense, Miss Brodie is also like the fascist leaders whom she so admires. Through her teaching she is able to manipulate her set and to attempt to indoctrinate them with her own misguided beliefs. Control is all important and she even encourages her girls to participate in actions which frighten her: Rose Douglas is groomed to have the love affair with Teddy Lloyd which she herself has renounced. Everything in life has to be fashioned in her own image, whatever the consequences.

At the end of the narrative, Miss Brodie's inability to understand the moral wickedness of her actions leads to her undoing. When Joyce Emily Hammond decides to run off to join her brother in the Spanish Civil War, Miss Brodie persuades her to join Franco's side, whereas most people were 'anti-Franco, if they were anything at all' (p. 118). When Sandy hears this story it gives her the confidence to tell Miss Mackay that Miss Brodie has been teaching fascism to her younger pupils.

That she herself is unaware of her own prejudices is made clear when she tells Sandy after the war that 'Hitler *was* rather naughty' (p. 122).

Childhood and adolescence

The novel is rooted firmly in the world of a girls' school and much of the action is seen through the eyes of the girls in Miss Brodie's set. When she first teaches them, they are ten-year-old girls in the junior school – impressionable and willing to embrace her particular style of teaching. It is made clear that this influence is distrusted by the other teachers who dislike both Miss Brodie and the girls whom she teaches. Although the girls subsequently grow away from Miss Brodie during the course of their education she retains a hold over them and still influences their development. Much of her control comes from her myth-making. She invents and then re-invents or refines the story of her idealised love for the talented Hugh Carruthers who was supposed to have been killed shortly before the end of the First World War. Through this story she is able to include elements of her own relationship with the teachers Teddy Lloyd and Gordon Lowther and to pass on coded messages to her pupils. Sandy in particular is fascinated by Miss Brodie's ability to create different stories out of the same set of facts.

However, the introduction of myth-making also provides the novel with some of its richest comic passages. In a mirror-image of Miss Brodie's heroic bathos about the doomed Hugh Carruthers, Sandy and Jenny compose their own romantic fiction around the story of Hugh, Miss Brodie and Lowther. Much of their interest lies in the sexual aspects of the relationship and in a final letter they imagine Miss Brodie and Lowther making love on Arthur's Seat in the middle of Edinburgh while a storm is raging. It is not enough for them to do it in an 'ordinary bed'.

Although the content of this passage is deliberately hilarious, there is a serious side to its inclusion in the novel. At the time Sandy, too, is engaged in living in a world of make-believe. Earlier, she has imagined herself in conversation with fictional characters like Alan Breck and Mr Rochester, but after Jenny meets a man exposing himself in public, her heated imagination centres on a policewoman making the enquiries. With her make-believe companion – whom Sandy calls 'Sergeant Anne Grey' – she dedicates herself to ridding 'sex from Edinburgh and environs' and that includes finding evidence of Miss Brodie's own relationship with Gordon Lowther. The concocted letter from Miss Brodie to him is part of the incriminating evidence demanded by the imaginary sergeant. The episode is presented as part of the girls' development – the papers are finally hidden on the seashore and forgotten – but the girls' fascination with mixing fact and fiction is a reflection of Sandy's real betrayal of Miss Brodie.

Before the onset of adolescence sexual fantasy takes up a substantial part of the girls' lives. They try, but fail to imagine the extent of Miss Brodie's sex life and when Monica Douglas reports seeing Teddy Lloyd kissing Miss Brodie this leads to further fevered imaginings. As they grow older pure sex becomes less important but it still informs their lives. They are aware of the extent of Miss Brodie's relationship with Gordon Lowther and they come to understand that she has rejected the attentions of Teddy Lloyd. Although Miss Brodie hopes that Rose will take her place in his bed, it is Sandy who eventually has a love affair with the art teacher.

However it is one of the book's many ironies that Miss Brodie's influence on her set is so short-lived: despite her teaching none of them is destined to reach their prime and all come to reject her doctrines. Sandy's is the most spectacular rejection because she not only turns to the Catholicism hated by Miss Brodie but she becomes a nun.

Language and style

The novel is not written from a first-person point of view but from the detached observation of a third party. In most novels of this kind, the observer describing the action can safely be described as the novelist but Muriel Spark has admitted that the author of the narrative has to be regarded as a character with a separate existence. In *The Prime of Miss Jean Brodie*, the narrator knows enough about Miss Brodie, the girls in her set and life at the Marcia Blaine School to assume that she, too, is part of the story and not a detached outsider.

From the opening sentence which describes the scene outside the Marcia Blaine School, Spark invites the reader to enter a world of her own creation and the device is continued throughout the novel to the concluding passage in which Sandy, now Sister Helena of the Transfiguration, is seen clutching desperately at her grille. Inventiveness and close observation are the keys to her literary style. This does not imply the over-use of adjectives to build up a rich or gaudy picture – on the contrary, Spark's prose is muscular and restrained – but it is one of the strengths of her writing that she is able to create scenes with the introduction of a few telling descriptions.

In no other episode is this ability seen to better advantage than the scene in Chapter 2 in which Miss Brodie takes her girls for a walk through the old parts of Edinburgh. It takes its cue from a flashforward in time in which Eunice remembers her childhood and opens with a simple rhetorical device: 'It is time now to speak of . . .' (p. 27). A spare description of the bitter winter weather sets the scene and a few economic physical descriptions of the girls and their demeanour. The portrayal is not just included for literary edification but adds to our understanding of their characters. Use is also made of poetic irony: Rose Stanley has a 'superficial knowledge' of Meccano sets and other 'boys' affairs', an understanding which is described as standing her 'in good stead a few years later with the boys'. Miss Brodie, of course, fails to understand this trait.

When the group reaches the Grassmarket – home to some of Edinburgh's worst slums – there is a marked contrast between their orderliness and the poverty and squalor around them. This is a real scene, based on Spark's knowledge of the area, and tellingly described, but it has also been transformed by Spark's poetic insights – it is worth recalling that she is also an accomplished poet. A man sits on the ice-cold pavement, boys shout obscene taunts, women in shawls appear from doorways: to the observant Sandy it is as if they have entered a foreign country where they are regarded as strangers. The juxtaposition of the scenes of destitution with the girls' utter incomprehension lends the aura of illusion to a vividly realised scene. In a telling flashforward during an interview with a man who was at school in Edinburgh at the same time, Sandy realises 'with a shock' that the past can have several interpretations and layers of meaning.

Reality is not always what it first seems to be and is actually a matter of perception: one person's idea of reality may be very different from someone else's.

The use of dialogue is also startlingly descriptive, especially in the case of Miss Brodie whose speech patterns betray the presence of a middle-class Edinburgh accent. (This is one reason why the dramatised version of the novel has been so successful: it allows an actress to take the Brodie character and impose upon it a distinct personality through her use of clipped and frequently pedantic speech.) Indeed, it is one of the novel's many pleasures that Spark infuses her characters with a good deal of humour, some of it based on Miss Brodie's pedantic tendency and some of it on the girls' juvenile misunderstandings. When Mary is discovered reading a comic book in class, not only is she too stupid to invent an excuse but she is also ridiculed. She describes it as a 'comic' which Miss Brodie chooses to interpret as a 'comedian', much to the girl's discomfort. When Sandy talks about Miss Brodie's 'prime', Jenny retorts that she remained unmarried, unlike her parents who have 'sexual intercourse'. When the girls are speaking no attempt is made to give them adult speech; rather, they speak and think as girls of their age and their insights reveal that they are in fact children and not young adults. Sandy is embarrassed by her mother's use of 'darling' instead of the more familiar Scottish endearment 'dear'.

The novel is also an evocation of the Edinburgh Spark knew as a child and it contains some vivid poetic descriptions, not just of the city but of the people who live there. Remembering a winter's day, she not only sees the greyness of the north but allows the reader to feel it: 'The wind blew from the icy Forth and the sky was loaded with forthcoming snow' (p. 27). At other times the grey city can be suddenly transformed; 'dark heavy Edinburgh itself could suddenly be changed into a floating city when the light was a special pearly white and fell upon one of the gracefully fashioned streets' (p. 111). A winter evening is evoked by a simple domestic event: 'The evening paper rattle-snaked its way through the letter box and there was suddenly a six-o'clock feeling in the house' (p. 21). The numbing poverty of unemployed men seen by the girls during a winter walk is underlined by a subtle observation: 'They were talking and spitting and smoking little bits of cigarette held between middle finger and thumb' (p. 39).

Literary allusions

The novel is rich in literary and biblical quotations. Whether or not they are attributed, there is good reason for their inclusion: Spark loads each one of them with hidden meanings which help to amplify the narration.

(1) P. 6: 'O where shall I find a virtuous woman, for her price is above rubies.' (Proverbs, 31:10). The text is taken from Lemuel's lesson of chastity and lists the requirements of a woman of true virtue. One of the injunctions could apply to Miss Brodie: 'She openeth her mouth with wisdom; and in her tongue is the law of kindness.' The juxtaposition is deliberately ironic: as a teacher Miss Brodie is charged with providing her pupils with a virtuous education – which on one level, she does – but she is also guilty of attempting to manipulate their lives, hardly the action of a 'virtuous woman'.

(2) Pp. 7 and 21: The Lady of Shalott. Although Sandy recites the lines from Tennyson's poem for the class's edification and for Miss Brodie's enjoyment of her 'vowel sounds', the Lady of Shalott is also an important part of Sandy's fantasy life. Not only does she bear a resemblance to Miss Brodie but it is also entirely in keeping that when Sandy asks how she came to write her name on the prow of the boat which takes her to Camelot, the Lady replies that it was done with a pot of paint which had been left behind by 'some heedless member of the Unemployed'.

The use of the lines and Sandy's obvious enjoyment of them is also a flashforward to her own future existence as a nun. Just as the Lady of Shalott lives within 'four grey towers' on a 'silent isle', so too does Sandy join a strict religious order cut off from the rest of the world.

(3) P. 12: 'Season of mists and mellow fruitfulness.' The opening lines of John Keats's poem 'To Autumn' are used by Miss Brodie to introduce the story of her beloved Hugh Carruthers who died in the last days of the First World War. On one level she quotes from the poem, but does not acknowledge its provenance because it is an autumn day and she is with her class outside on the school's lawn, but, as with everything Miss Brodie does, there is more to the action than first meets the eye.

The poem is Keats's last major work and was written shortly before his death at the early age of twenty-six. In that respect Miss Brodie is making a conscious comparison between Hugh who 'fell like an autumn leaf' and the early death of Keats. The poem itself is an elegy for the passing of summer and the transience of life but it has always been associated with early death.

Miss Brodie continues the conceit by referring to Hugh as one of the 'Flowers of the Forest': the original lament was for the dead at the Battle of Flodden in 1517 but she connects it to Hugh's death in Flanders. As the novel progresses Sandy notices Miss Brodie's ability to embellish and change the story to suit her own purposes.

(4) Pp. 28–30, 37: Alan Breck and *Kidnapped*. It is entirely apposite that Sandy's fantasy life should embrace the character of Alan Breck Stewart from the novel by Robert Louis Stevenson. Like the Lady of Shalott, though in different ways, he bears a resemblance to Miss

Brodie. At the time Sandy is escaping from the reality of a school walk in which she has to accompany the despised Mary Macgregor, but in her childish way she is also musing on her love for Miss Brodie.

In Stevenson's novel Alan Breck is a romantic adventurer who plays fast and loose with the restraints of everyday life. To the novel's other main character, the staid Lowlander David Balfour, he is an invigorating and life-enhancing influence. Although Sandy cannot articulate that feeling for Miss Brodie, by fantasising about Alan Breck she is subconsciously making the connection between the fictional hero and her teacher. The comparison is given an ironic edge when Sandy says: 'I shall never fail you, Alan Breck. Never.' By the novel's end she has, of course, betrayed Miss Brodie.

Within Spark's novel the cautious music teacher Gordon Lowther resembles David Balfour while the more dashing artist Teddy Lloyd can be seen as an Alan Breck-type character.

(5) P. 38: 'Kilmeny was pure as pure could be.' The line from James Hogg's poem 'Kilmeny' is used by Miss Brodie to describe Hugh's pureness of mind and body although it is also possible that she is referring to her own condition prior to her affair with Gordon Lowther. In the poem Kilmeny is described as a 'virgin in her prime'.

Kilmeny tells the story of a young virgin of the same name who is removed for seven years to another world, where she is bathed in the stream of life before being taken to a green mountain and shown examples of human wickedness in the vision of the lady with the lion and the 'untoward bedeman' – a reference to Mary Queen of Scots and the reformer John Knox – and the lion and the eagle – a reference to the French Revolution. At the end of the poem she asks the spirits to send her back to her own country to tell her tale, but earth cannot hold her and she returns to the spirit world of beauty and tranquillity.

The reference to 'Kilmeny' is further evidence of Miss Brodie's dual personality. She wants to be considered virtuous and other-worldly like Kilmeny, but in reality her life is dominated by her ambition for her girls and far from being a virgin she is involved in a clandestine relationship with Gordon Lowther.

(6) P. 47: 'Come autumn sae pensive, in yellow and gray,/And soothe me wi' tidings o'nature's decay.' The lines from Robert Burns's song 'My Nanie's Awa'' are uttered by Miss Brodie at the end of the summer holidays when the girls are back at school. Like the lines from Keats, they are reminders of death and the passing of time.

In Burns's song they are also a lament for lost love and refer indirectly to Miss Brodie's own relationships – not just with Hugh Carruthers but also her unconsummated love for Teddy Lloyd. It is interesting to note that the more Miss Brodie discusses Hugh, the more similar he is to Robert Burns – his love of poetry, his Ayrshire home and his educated, though poverty-stricken, background. Burns, too, died at an early age, when he was only thirty-seven.

(7) P. 58: Mr Rochester and *Jane Eyre*: Sandy's other fictional fantasy involves Edward Fairfax Rochester, the Byronic hero of Charlotte Brontë's novel. Although Sandy uses the device to compare Miss Gaunt to the character of the housekeeper, her fantasies about Rochester are in keeping with her own sexuality.

Throughout the novel we are reminded that Sandy is unattractive and there are constant references to her small piggy eyes. Jane Eyre, too, is described as being plain yet the handsome and sardonic Rochester is smitten enough by her to want to marry her. In similar fashion Teddy Lloyd turns down Rose Stanley 'famous for sex' in favour of an affair with Sandy whom he describes, unkindly, as 'just about the ugliest little thing I've ever seen in my life' (p. 102).

Characters

One of the novel's great strengths is Spark's creation of a gallery of seductive and totally believable characters. For all her faults – and they are many – Jean Brodie manages to retain the reader's interests and affection, simply because she is such a human creation. Similarly the girls are portrayed unsentimentally and straightforwardly as if they, too, were drawn from life. There is no attempt to glamorise them and they are presented as a group of normal schoolgirls who could be found at any school in any part of the country.

While Miss Brodie and the girls in her set are strongly drawn and realised, the supporting characters have a more sketchy existence but that does not mean that they are inconsequential or do not have roles to play. The naming of Miss Gaunt is evidence of Spark's liking for providing characters with suitably descriptive surnames. She is simply introduced as a forbidding spinster who dislikes both Miss Brodie and her girls. Similarly, the economic description of the two sewing mistresses, Ellen and Alison Kerr, is sufficient to place them: 'they were incapable of imparting any information whatsoever, so flustered were they, with their fluffed-out hair, dry blue-grey skins and birds' eyes' (p. 54).

Muriel Spark is not a feminist writer but it is interesting to note that both the male characters, Teddy Lloyd and Gordon Lowther, are weak and easily dominated by females. Lowther remains in awe of his long-dead mother and it is obvious that Deirdre Lloyd has the measure of her philandering artist husband. It is only natural that both men should be easily dominated by Miss Brodie – Lowther by surrendering to her domestic regime and Lloyd by allowing all his portraits to resemble her. When he tells Sandy he would like to paint all the Brodie girls she replies, 'We'd look like one big Miss Brodie, I suppose' (p. 102).

Miss Jean Brodie

Muriel Spark has admitted in her autobiography *Curriculum Vitae* that there was a real-life model for Miss Jean Brodie. During her schooldays at James Gillespie's School in Edinburgh she was taught by a Miss Christina Kay, whom she describes as a 'character in search of an author'. While no fictional character is ever based completely on one single model, having been transformed by the literary process, there are many points of comparison between Miss Kay and Miss Brodie: an interest in Italian Renaissance art, a fondness for travel, an exhilarating teaching style, even the catchphrase 'crème de la crème'.

Jean Brodie is one of the great characters of modern fiction and it says much for Spark's realisation of her that she has transferred so successfully to the stage and screen in Jay Presson Allen's dramatisation of the novel. For many readers, Jean Brodie exists as a real person and others claim that they, too, have encountered teachers like her.

Her surname is the key to her character. Spark admits she got it from a family friend who had been a schoolteacher and whose maiden name it was, but there is little doubt that she chose it deliberately. Jean Brodie claims to be a descendant of Deacon William Brodie, the eighteenth-century Edinburgh burgess who led a double life, upright citizen by day and thief by night. Like that famous forebear, Jean Brodie also leads two lives. On the one hand, in reality, she believes herself to be a devout Edinburgh spinster and committed teacher; on the other, in her imagination, she sees herself as a doomed romantic heroine – her fictional relationship with Hugh Carruthers is an extension of this belief. She is both the author and the creation of this imaginary world.

There are other paradoxes. She claims to have sacrificed her life and her career for her girls but whenever circumstances do not suit her she attempts to change them to her advantage, even if that means using her girls to carry out her will. While she teaches the importance of individuality and reminds her class that safety does not come first, she is a moral coward who incites others into acts she dare not commit herself. In that sense much of her life is lived in her own mind and she has little conception of the consequences for others of her own actions.

In appearance her good looks and fashionable dress sense are compared with the dowdiness of her contemporary colleagues – the sporting Miss Lockhart is an exception – and Spark goes to considerable pains to underline her 'Roman' looks. She is described as having a 'dark Roman profile', which Hugh much admired and even in retirement she is seen as a 'Roman matron'. Her set also see her as Julius Caesar when she is under threat from the headmistress: 'If the authorities wanted to get rid of her she would have to be assassinated' (p. 9). Partly the description fits her because she has a love for Italy and its culture but there is another side to the allusion to Rome. Like Julius Caesar, Miss Brodie is also betrayed by those closest to her.

Sandy Stranger

Again the deliberate choice of surname is a clue to the girl's character. Sandy is a natural outsider, an observer who watches life and does not fully participate in it. She is 'the stranger' in the set who becomes Miss Brodie's eyes and ears: that relationship is cemented towards the end of the novel when Miss Brodie declares that the sixteen-year-old Sandy should become a Secret Service agent or a spy. The fact that she is always described as having small or non-existent eyes is an ironic comment on her anomalous position within the set: her eyes might be tiny but they are all-seeing. Throughout the novel she is described as being the least attractive member of the Brodie set and there are several references to the smallness of those eyes.

Despite her lack of good looks Sandy is also the character who resembles Miss Brodie most closely. In her childhood years she admits to loving Miss Brodie and she fantasises about her and her relationships in the story she creates with Jenny. Later, she even takes Miss Brodie's place when she becomes Teddy Lloyd's lover. Picked out as the most intelligent of the girls – all the members of the Brodie set have special mannerisms or attributes – she also leads a double life, indulging in the romantic fantasies which prevent her from becoming bored. She is also half-English and half-Scottish; and therefore, like Miss Brodie, has a split personality. And that divided self is continued to the novel's conclusion when she adopts a new religion and another name – Sister Helena of the Transfiguration. This is the final result of her retreat from everyday reality. Schooled in Miss Brodie's beliefs in predestination, Sandy eventually rejects them by exercising free will. However, it is one of the novel's many ironies that Sandy's decision to renounce Miss Brodie's ideology imprisons her within a new faith in which she 'found quite a number of Fascists much less agreeable than Miss Brodie' (p. 125).

Monica Douglas

Famous for 'being able to do real mathematics in her head, and for her anger' (p. 27), Monica also has a specific physical description which is repeated during the novel. She has 'a very red nose, winter and summer, long dark plaits and fat, peg-like legs' (p. 6), and her latent anger can be seen in her 'dark red face' (p. 27). Spark is obviously not afraid of making her characters appear physically unattractive.

She plays two minor, though important, roles in the narrative. First she sees Jean Brodie kissing Teddy Lloyd and reports the incident to the rest of the set, thereby arousing their interest in sex in general and in Miss Brodie's love life in particular. Secondly, in later life, it is to Monica that Miss Brodie confides her suspicion that Sandy was the one who finally betrayed her to the school authorities. Miss Brodie might have left the Marcia Blaine School but she continues to exert an influence over her favoured pupils.

Rose Stanley

A pretty blonde girl with an arresting profile, Rose is selected by Jean Brodie as her surrogate for a love affair with Teddy Lloyd. However, while the art teacher admires her as a model, he is not attracted to her. Although Rose is described as being 'famous for sex', Spark also makes it clear that this is in fact not the case and that her sex appeal is limited to her good looks: 'she did not really talk about sex, far less indulge it' (p. 110). Of all the girls in the set, she and the worldly Eunice are the least interested in talking about or understanding Miss Brodie's sexual relationships.

In keeping with an inability to perceive reality, though, Miss Brodie does not understand Rose, and prefers to keep alive the fiction that by becoming Lloyd's model she and the art teacher will soon be lovers. Miss Brodie makes much of Rose's 'instincts', believing them to be those of a beautiful and sexually liberated girl, a match for Teddy Lloyd's artistic inspiration. In fact Rose's instincts tell her to be satisfied with the role of Lloyd's model and to avoid any emotional involvement with him.

Spark also hints that Rose has a fixation on her bluff hearty father, a widower, who is 'as handsome in his masculine way as was Rose in her feminine' (p. 119). Miss Brodie fails to understand that side of Rose's personality, and imagines that when she is seventeen or eighteen she will be fulfilled sexually. Of all the girls in the set Rose is the least understood by her friends and Miss Brodie, and it is entirely typical of her 'instincts' that she should marry a man like her father soon after she leaves school. And having thrown off her schooldays, 'she shook off Miss Brodie's influence as a dog shakes pond-water from its coat' (p. 119).

Eunice Gardiner

Although she plays a relatively minor role and is one of the lesser members of the set – she is so quiet that it is difficult to see what contribution she can make – Eunice provides a number of keys for understanding the workings of Miss Brodie's personality and mind. She is a good gymnast who does cartwheels for the amusement of the class, but this is not allowed on Sundays, 'for in many ways Miss Brodie was an Edinburgh spinster of the deepest dye'.

Eunice also acts as an unwitting foil to Miss Brodie's pedantic insistence on correct linguistic and grammatical usage. As a girl she is reprimanded by Miss Brodie for using the adjective 'social' as a noun (p. 62) but later in life, as a married woman, she continues the error in conversation with her husband. She tells him that Miss Brodie used to talk about being in her 'prime'. Her husband replies: 'Prime what?' While Spark is indulging in a mild verbal joke, she is also revealing how little Eunice has been touched by Miss Brodie's teaching.

In fact Eunice was always the set's most unlikely member. Miss Brodie does her best to encourage her to think of greater things in life and to find a vocation, otherwise she will end up a Girl Guide. This is meant as a dire warning, but Eunice is secretly attracted by the idea. A member of Miss Brodie's set she might be, but she still retains control over her own preferences. Again, the message seems to be that although Miss Brodie's influence is great when the girls are young, it has little lasting effect on their lives.

Mary Macgregor

The first mention of Mary Macgregor is the key to understanding her character: she is 'a nobody whom everybody could blame' (p. 8). A natural butt of Miss Brodie's sarcasm, the girl whom nobody likes, it is Mary's fate to be one of life's losers. Even her premature death is as much farce as tragedy. In a flashforward at the start of Chapter 2, Spark reveals that she dies in a hotel fire in Cumberland during the Second World War, running backwards and forwards in a vain attempt to escape. The inference is that she was too clumsy and too stupid and always had been – the flashforward is occasioned by Miss Brodie accusing her of spilling ink on the floor in class.

Taking their lead from their teacher's example, the other girls also taunt Mary. Sandy is particularly guilty of this failing. She provides Mary with the wrong answer to respond to Miss Brodie and during the walk through Edinburgh she is deliberately unpleasant to her. Although her instinct is to be kind, the fear of breaking the group's solidarity prevents her and she is deliberately cruel. This is an uncomfortable reference to the theory of the Calvinist elect: far better to be a member, even a stupid one, than to be outside the group. In that sense Sandy sees that Mary is 'at least inside Miss Brodie's category of heroines in the making' (p. 30).

Mary has to pay a high price for belonging to the Brodie set. She is humiliated by her teacher and teased by her fellow pupils; she thinks Latin is the same as shorthand and believes that Caesar's Gallic Wars date from the time of Samuel Pepys; she suggests that poor people are dirty because they do not send their clothes to a laundry; she is even 'too stupid to have any sex-wits of her own' (p. 50), and throughout the novel she remains unaware of the extent of Miss Brodie's relationships.

And yet, in spite of these sleights, Mary is the most loyal of Miss Brodie's group. She refuses to speak badly of her when the headmistress attempts to befriend her, 'thinking her to be gullible and bribable' (p. 77), and at the end of her short life she continues to hold to the belief that her days with Miss Brodie gave her the happiest time of her life.

Of all the girls in the set Mary requires the most help and attention from her teacher but she is constantly ignored and reviled. It is one of the novel's many ironies that Mary is betrayed by her mentor even though she is presented as a suitable case for Miss Brodie's educational theories.

Miss Mackay

The headmistress of the Marcia Blaine School spends a good deal of effort and energy in attempting to dislodge Miss Brodie from her job. She dislikes her methods of teaching even though these are hardly radical. Although she is presented as an elderly and forbidding figure – Rose describes her as having 'an awfully red face, with all the veins showing' – she is in fact younger than Miss Brodie and has better educational qualifications, a fact which Miss Brodie acknowledges.

Whenever she interviews the girls she attempts to find evidence which will incriminate Miss Brodie. Mary Macgregor is befriended in the hope that, being stupid, she will provide the necessary information. But when Miss Brodie's nightdress is found by the Kerr sisters in Gordon Lowther's bed, she decides that it is insufficient evidence. This information she imparts to Sandy Stranger when the time comes for Miss Brodie's betrayal. Spark underscores Miss Mackay's essential conservatism by describing her distaste at the brutal way in which Sandy says that she is 'putting a stop to Miss Brodie'.

Teddy Lloyd

Like Miss Brodie, the school's art teacher is based on a real-life character: Arthur Couling whom the girls at Muriel Spark's school thought handsome and glamorous. Although there are no physical similarities between the real art teacher and his fictional counterpart, Spark has admitted that the incident in which Teddy Lloyd smashes a saucer in exasperation did happen in one of Couling's painting classes.

Lloyd has lost his arm in the First World War and this provides a point of connection with Hugh, who may or may not have existed as Miss Brodie's lost fiancé. As she tells the girls, he was a natural artist who was killed in Flanders at the end of the First World War before his gifts could be realised. Although Lloyd survived the war, he is married, with a large family; this and his Catholic faith deter Miss Brodie from having a relationship with him. Her refusal mirrors the fact that her love affair with

Hugh was stillborn, and allows her to transform that reality into the myth of her doomed love.

However, despite Miss Brodie's unwillingness to enter into a love affair, Lloyd is obviously besotted with her, and Sandy quickly notices that he cannot paint any portraits without making them in Miss Brodie's likeness. He remains in love with her even though he knows that she will never reciprocate his feelings. For that reason his affair with Sandy, Miss Brodie's surrogate, is the only way in which he can get close to her.

Deirdre Lloyd

Although a minor character – her appearance is limited to Chapter 5 – Teddy's wife represents the kind of artistic licence which Miss Brodie professes to admire but could never practise. She wears attractive 'peasant' clothes which add to her artistic appeal and she is a natural liberal. With all her children and her gipsy dress she could be a 'Mother Earth' figure, but Spark makes clear that she is an attractive woman who is secure in her marriage, despite her husband's obvious infatuation with Miss Brodie.

Gordon Lowther

The school's music teacher is physically similar to Teddy Lloyd – both are described as being 'red gold in colouring' – but emotionally and mentally he is very different. From an early stage it is made clear that he is easily dominated by women. Not only did he live with his widowed mother until her death but still reacts as if she watches his every move. The girls notice that he touches everything in his own home as if he is not allowed to do anything without his mother's – and now Miss Brodie's – permission.

When the two sewing mistresses are foisted on him as his housekeepers he does not object and he gives in lamely when Miss Gaunt uses her influence to make him give up his post as elder of the local Church of Scotland where her brother is the minister. And just as lamely he falls under Miss Brodie's spell. (Spark does not provide specific details about their affair but it is implicit that Miss Brodie is the dominant partner.) Although she becomes his lover she refuses to marry him, a state of affairs which he finds uncomfortable. In order to marry and to regain his position in Edinburgh society he eventually proposes to, and is accepted by, Miss Lockhart, the school's chemistry teacher who is presented as a far more suitable choice. This gives him the respectability which he craves but which Miss Brodie refuses to provide. Unable to sustain his secret relationship with Miss Brodie he opts for the safety of a conventional marriage.

Part 4

Hints for study

When preparing for an examination, your knowledge of the text is all-important. While it is useful to read critical commentaries on the novel in particular, or on the work of Muriel Spark in general (see 'Suggestions for further reading'), nothing is better than an intimate understanding of the work in question. An examiner will be more impressed by evidence of your knowledge of the novel than with a repetition of what other critics have written about it.

Reading the text

The novel is short enough to be read at a single sitting. This should be done for pleasure and to get a feeling for Muriel Spark's distinctive prose style. Although there is no need to take notes at this stage it should be possible to identify the main themes, recognise the principal characters and understand the background against which the action takes place. Note that the novel is not being told from a stated person's point of view, but is reported narrative, that is, the story unfolds through its telling by an unseen but all-knowing narrator.

Once this has been done, it is a good idea to spend some time reflecting on the novel's contents and the ways in which the story is told. Because the novel is not told as a continuous narrative, it is important to pick out and identify the use of flashbacks and flashforwards. This exercise is particularly helpful because the characters and their motives are only gradually revealed to the reader. Remember, too, that although this novel contains several serious themes there is also a good deal of fun: allow yourself to laugh at some of the more preposterous episodes and the author's sustained use of irony. A novel should be enjoyable as well as instructive.

The next stage is to read the novel for a second time, this time taking notes. At this point you should know what you want from your notes: these will be your main tools when you are revising for an examination and they must make sense. Working through the novel slowly and deliberately you should make notes under headings such as: the main characters, physical descriptions, time-scale, themes (see Commentary for further suggestions), and use of language. Noting page numbers will make future reference easier. It will also make sense to write a brief summary to keep beside you while you are reading through the novel. This will help you to understand the use of flashbacks and flashforwards in the revelation of character development and motives for their actions.

Take time to examine the language of the novel and to note the ways in which Spark carefully chooses her words. For example, the religious allusions are important: the girls are described as 'disciples' and Miss Brodie does not simply give up her love for Teddy Lloyd, she 'renounces' him. Try to work out if the dialogues are true to life or seem artificial? Are there times when Miss Brodie seems to be discussing arguments which her pupils cannot possibly understand because they are still too young and immature?

To illustrate your main argument within an essay you should commit to memory a small number of quotations from the novel. Not only will this demonstrate a familiarity with the text but the use of extracts can help convince the examiner that you understand the question and are confident about your own response. There is no need to memorise large chunks of the novel – and do not use quotations unless you are certain that they are word-perfect – but memorising a limited number of short, apposite extracts may prove extremely useful. For example, Miss Brodie's personality and characteristics can be summed up economically in Spark's description of her as she is seen by the girls of her set at any early stage in the novel: 'She looked a mighty woman with her dark Roman profile in the sun.'

Preparing for an examination

Once you have made sure that you are fully conversant with the text and have completed a full set of notes, you should attempt to write an essay from the following list of questions. Although it will be impossible to replicate the exact conditions of an examination you should try to write an essay within the time and space limits imposed by a formal examination.

Before attempting to answer a question, make sure that you understand it and that you feel sufficiently confident to answer it. Never attempt a question if you are doubtful about what is required from it. The length of a question is not always a guide to its complexity. For example a short and apparently simple question often requires a precise response and you will lose marks if you stray from the main point or if you pad out the essay with extraneous information. Equally, a question which makes a general point usually demands the demonstration of a broader general knowledge of the novel and the writer's technique.

Once you have decided which question to answer, draw up a brief plan or outline. Do not spend too much time doing this and do not over-elaborate: the main necessity is to concentrate on writing the essay within the time that is available to you. The plan, though, will provide a point of reference and will help you to focus on the question. Once started, the essay should be introduced by a statement which considers the question and makes clear to what extent you agree with it. (Do not be afraid to disagree with the point being posed by the examiner, but you must be prepared to back up your comments by reference to the text.) The main text of the essay is the discussion of your argument and it should be completed by a summary and conclusion. Do not attempt to write too much: 1,000 words should be enough to cover the salient points.

Once you have finished, re-read the essay carefully and examine it against the outline. Check the spelling of the names of all the characters and the proper nouns: errors of this kind will suggest unfamiliarity with the text and you will lose marks. Also ask yourself if you have really understood the question and answered it correctly.

Other reading

Although the main point of the examination is to test your understanding of *The Prime of Miss Jean Brodie*, you may enjoy looking at some of Muriel Spark's other novels. (See 'Suggestions for further reading'.) It is interesting, for example, to examine the character of Patrick Seton in *The Comforters*: like Miss Brodie he sees the world in his own image and cannot understand the moral ambiguities of his own actions. When his girl friend becomes pregnant he refuses to acknowledge that fact and even contemplates murder as a means of denying harsh reality. On the subject of religious conversion, *The Girls of Slender Means* examines the process which leads Sandy and Nicholas Farringdon into the Catholic church. Like Sandy Stranger, they, too, have to reject other creeds before fully accepting their new faith.

The theme of the dual personality takes centre place in *The Ballad of Peckham Rye* in which the diabolic Dougal Douglas plays havoc with the people of Peckham. Like Gil-martin in Hogg's *Private Memoirs and Confessions of a Justified Sinner* he has the alarming ability to change his appearance at will and appears in several different guises throughout the novel. No one who meets him is left unaffected by the experience and he has the disconcerting ability to discover in them a 'fatal flaw' which he exploits to his own evil advantage. Like Jean Brodie, Dougal Douglas is a Scot from Edinburgh and like her, too, he enjoys interfering in the lives of the others, usually to their disadvantage.

If you want to be more ambitious you should take time to read or at least look at some of the other literary works to which allusions have been made in the text. You may already have read Charlotte Brontë's novel *Jane Eyre* or Robert Louis Stevenson's *Kidnapped*, and it will not be difficult to read Alfred, Lord Tennyson's 'The Lady of Shalott', John Keats's 'To Autumn' or Robert Burns's 'My Nanie's Awa''.

Later, to understand more fully the theme of the divided personality in Scottish fiction, you might like to read James Hogg's novel *The Private Memoirs and Confessions of a Justified Sinner*. Although much of the dialogue is written in Scots it is an entertaining book which rewards the reader with its keen insights into the idea that sins committed by an elect and justified person cannot imperil the hope of salvation. Perhaps the most celebrated work of fiction on dual personality in world literature, is also by a native of Edinburgh, Robert Louis Stevenson's: *The Strange Case of Dr Jekyll and Mr Hyde* (also based on the character of Deacon Brodie – see above, p. 9). Critics and biographers have also attributed the darker side of Stevenson's writing to the influence of Calvinism (see pp. 56–7 below).

If you make reference to any other texts within your answer, do not devote too much space to them: the examiner is primarily concerned with your knowledge and understanding of *The Prime of Miss Jean Brodie*.

Specimen questions

(1) Miss Brodie calls her girls the 'crème de la crème'. Are they really different from their fellow pupils?

(2) Discuss the use of flashbacks and flashforwards in the novel.

(3) What is the importance of the Edinburgh background to *The Prime of Miss Jean Brodie*?

(4) Is Sandy Stranger being honest when she gives her reasons for betraying Miss Brodie?

(5) How does Miss Brodie attempt to change reality to suit her own purposes?

(6) 'She thinks she is Providence, thought Sandy, she thinks she is the God of Calvin, she sees the beginning and the end.' Is this a fair assessment of Miss Brodie?

(7) Explain the reasons for Sandy's conversion to Catholicism.

(8) In what sense can *The Prime of Miss Jean Brodie* be described as a Scottish novel?

(9) Because none of Miss Jean Brodie's girls ever reaches their prime, her influence as a teacher is a failure. Is this true?

(10) Show how Muriel Spark uses historical reality to create the fictional world inhabited by Miss Brodie and her set of girls.

(11) 'For all her admiration for Miss Brodie, Spark makes fun of her fantasies.' Discuss.

(12) Discuss Muriel Spark's use of literary references in *The Prime of Miss Jean Brodie*.

(13) Compare and contrast the double lives led by Miss Brodie and Sandy Stranger.

(14) Explain how Sandy discovers the relationship between Miss Brodie's set and Calvinism.

Specimen answers

(2) Discuss the use of flashbacks and flashforwards in *The Prime of Miss Jean Brodie*.

Muriel Spark does not use a conventional chronology in *The Prime of Miss Jean Brodie* with a beginning, a middle and an ending. Instead the narrative is punctuated by flashbacks and flashforwards in time which allow the reader to understand why certain characters have developed in certain ways.

This is particularly true of the character Mary Macgregor. Introduced as a silly and ineffectual girl who is teased by her friends and scorned by Miss Brodie, it is revealed at the beginning of Chapter 2 that she dies in a hotel fire in Cumberland during the Second World War. The flashforward is introduced to explain why she believed that her time in Miss Brodie's class was the happiest period of her life. This is deeply ironic: Mary is a victim, yet, early in the novel, the reader knows that she will go to her death without understanding her appalling treatment at the hands of a teacher who is supposed to care for her.

In fact the use of different layers of time has already been indicated in the first chapter. The novel opens when the girls are sixteen yet it closes with a flashback when the girls are ten. Both actions are reported by an unseen narrator and the device is an economical method of allowing the reader to gain a comprehensive understanding of the main characters. For example, Miss Brodie's hold over her girls and her interest in their development at the age of sixteen are explained by the flashback to 1931, the year when they first encountered Miss Brodie.

The scene takes place during a history lesson beneath a tree on the school lawn. Instead of teaching the girls a proper history lesson, Miss Brodie tells them about her lost love Hugh, who died fighting during the First World War. Not only is this unusual in itself but it underlines the strength of the personal relationship between Miss Brodie and her girls. Thus, within the first dozen pages, Muriel Spark has managed to convey why the sixteen-year-old girls find Miss Brodie so attractive a personality.

The flashbacks to the first period of Miss Brodie's influence over her set are described at length and are relatively straightforward. Most of Chapter 2 is set in 1931 and contains an important description of a walk through Edinburgh. Not only is this colourful in itself but it also includes Sandy's insight that there is a link between Miss Brodie's admiration for fascism and the creation of her own 'set' – as she calls the girls.

In contrast, the flashforwards are usually brief and are introduced to provide essential information for the reader. For example, in Chapter 2, there is a jump forward to a later date when Eunice Gardiner is married. While talking to her husband about Miss Brodie and her 'prime', she reveals the fact that Miss Brodie was 'betrayed by one of her own girls'. At this stage the identity of the betrayer is not revealed and it is only half way through the novel that Sandy is named.

The chapter also includes a flashforward to Sandy Stranger's later life as Sister Helena of the Transfiguration. She is visited by an academic who had also been brought up in Edinburgh at the same time. While he reflects on the city's architectural beauty, Sandy can only remember the squalor she had seen during the walk through Edinburgh with Miss Brodie.

Chapter 3 deals with the second year of Miss Brodie's influence, and it, too, is punctuated by the use of jumps forward in time. There are two related incidents from a future date which relate to Miss Brodie's emotional life. First, Monica Douglas insists to Sandy, now a nun, that she did see Miss Brodie kissing the art teacher Teddy Lloyd – at the time the girls had been unwilling to believe her. Secondly, Miss Brodie confides in Sandy that Lloyd was indeed the love of her life. Because this chapter concentrates on the girls' sexual awakening, the flashforwards underline the emotional tensions within Miss Brodie's personal relationships. The second flashforward also reveals the truth about Sandy's betrayal of Miss Brodie. In both cases Muriel Spark is providing information which clarifies and amplifies the behaviour of her characters.

Flashbacks are widely used in fiction to give brief glimpses of the past which help the reader to understand the present. In *The Prime of Miss Jean Brodie* the first flashback to 1930 is continued in Chapters 2, 3 and 4 to bring the reader back to the time of the opening pages of the novel. The last chapter telescopes the action to include Sandy's affair with Teddy Lloyd and the final betrayal of Miss Brodie.

However, the use of the flashforward is the more interesting device because it allows the reader to understand the consequences of the characters' actions. On one level the time-scale of the novel embraces the years when the girls are at school and under Miss Brodie's influence. On another level, though, the use of flashforwards allows us to understand at an early stage that Sandy betrayed Miss Brodie, converted to Catholicism and, later, became a nun.

All this information is provided with considerable economy and it is one of Muriel Spark's gifts as a novelist that she releases the information at appropriate points in the narrative. The use of flashbacks and flashforwards are therefore central to her literary style.

---

(4) Is Sandy Stranger being honest when she gives her reasons for betraying Miss Brodie?

When Sandy Stranger betrays Miss Brodie to Miss Mackay she claims that she is only interested in 'putting a stop' to her activities. On one level this is true: she has firm political grounds for her decision. Throughout the novel Miss Brodie has never made any secret of her admiration for the fascists and with the war against Nazi Germany approaching, Sandy sees it as her duty to tell the school authorities about Miss Brodie's political convictions.

Sandy has also been upset by the death of one of her former classmates, Joyce Emily Hammond, who has been killed in the Spanish Civil War. Miss Brodie admits that she encouraged Joyce to follow her brother to the fighting without understanding that he was serving on the communist side. Instead, Miss Brodie has encouraged Joyce to fight for General Franco's right-wing Falangists.

As a result Miss Brodie is asked to leave the Marcia Blaine School and Miss Mackay the headmistress informs her that it was one of her own group who betrayed her. Throughout the novel, in flashforwards to future events, Miss Brodie constantly wonders who betrayed her before being told that it was in fact her favourite, Sandy Stranger.

However, on another level, this is not true and Sandy is being hypocritical when she tells Miss Mackay that the school authorities will not be able to sack her because of her sexual relationships. Sandy knows that Miss Brodie has been having an affair with the school's music teacher Mr Lowther but chooses not to provide the evidence. Instead she offers information about Miss Brodie's misguided admiration for fascism.

From an early stage in the novel Sandy realises the strength of Miss Brodie's concerns. Her girls are meant to share her artistic interests and she constantly praises the achievements of Mussolini's fascist government in Italy. As a consequence she insists that the girls should follow her advice and copy her interests. In time, as she grows up and develops intellectually, Sandy comes to believe that Miss Brodie is the embodiment of the strict protestantism which she herself comes to reject. In Miss Brodie she sees the concept of the 'elect' – those who believe that their actions are justified because they have an assured place in heaven.

However, Sandy either remains unaware of the real reasons for her betrayal or chooses not to face up to them. In an attempt to come to terms with her actions she has already told Miss Brodie that betrayal was impossible. If Miss Brodie did not betray the girls in her set then, in turn, they could not have betrayed her. This, too, is not true and Muriel Spark makes clear her doubts by describing Sandy's explanation as coming from an 'enigmatic Pope'.

In fact, Sandy is doubly guilty of betraying Miss Brodie. In her private life she betrays Miss Brodie's trust by having an affair with the school's art teacher Mr Lloyd whom Miss Brodie really loves. Then she compounds the action by turning to Catholicism, the religion which Miss Brodie detests. Sandy regards her betrayal as justified, yet it brings her no happiness.

Later still she becomes a nun in a reclusive order. She also achieves some fame as the author of a psychological treatise, but it is clear that none of these changes to her life brings her any contentment. Whenever her old school friends or other admirers visit her in her cell, she is portrayed as clutching the grille and acting in an agitated, almost feverish way. This suggests that she is ill at ease with her earlier act of betrayal.

(7) Explain the reasons for Sandy's conversion to Catholicism.

Conversion to the Roman Catholic faith is one of the main themes of *The Prime of Miss Jean Brodie* and a central concern of much of Muriel Spark's fiction. Having been brought up in a protestant background in Scotland, the author converted to Catholicism later in life and several of her fictional characters also undergo, or have undergone, a religious conversion.

While it is dangerous to read facts from an author's life into their fiction, it is interesting to understand that, like Sandy Stranger, Muriel Spark was brought up in Calvinist Edinburgh, grew up to understand its strengths and weaknesses and then became a Catholic. The understanding comes to Sandy when she is standing outside the church of St Giles – the principal presbyterian church in the city and a symbol of the protestant faith. Here, amidst Edinburgh's long history she contemplates the theory of predestination, by which members of the elect are promised eternal salvation. In this belief she sees the real importance of Miss Brodie's grip on her pupils: like the elect, the 'crème de la crème' are separated from the rest of the school by their adherence to Miss Brodie's philosophy.

However, it is not just Sandy's understanding of this connection, and her rejection of it, that leads to her conversion. It is Miss Brodie's perversion of the doctrine. She leads two lives and attempts to lead one of them vicariously through her pupils. Too timid to enter into a love affair with the romantic art teacher Teddy Lloyd, she attempts to groom one of her pupils, Rose Stanley, for the role of surrogate lover. When Sandy realises what is happening she gets her first inkling of Miss Brodie's need to manipulate their lives: 'She thinks she is Providence, thought Sandy, she thinks she is the God of Calvin, she sees the beginning and the end.'

More than any other insight, this perversion of Christian doctrine leads Sandy to want to put a stop to Miss Brodie's activities. Politics is used as an excuse when Miss Brodie's fascination for fascism leads her to encourage a pupil, Joyce Emily Hammond, to go off to the Spanish Civil War, where she is killed, but the real reason for Sandy's betrayal is her desire to deal with Miss Brodie's increasingly fanatical beliefs.

In the end it is Sandy who has the affair with Teddy Lloyd, thereby setting herself up as rival. When the affair ends she leaves him but takes his religion. Having left school she embraces Catholicism and, later still, becomes a nun in a strict religious order. By so doing she accepts a brand of religion which is as overwhelming as Calvinism. The suggestion seems to be that she has done this in penance for her act of betrayal. Certainly, the novel ends on an ambiguous note with Sandy, now Sister Helena of the Transfiguration and a bestselling author, clutching the bars of her cell and admitting to one of her visitors that the greatest influence on her life was 'a Miss Jean Brodie in her prime'.

---

(10) Show how Muriel Spark uses historical reality to create the fictional world inhabited by Miss Brodie and her set of girls.

The Prime of Miss Jean Brodie is firmly rooted in time and place and both elements play an important part in our understanding of the novel.

In fact, the novel has a definite time-scale: it opens in 1936, when the girls are in senior school, flashes back to 1930 when they first come under her influence and ends in 1938 when Sandy betrays Jean Brodie. Using a technique of taking the action forward, Muriel Spark also includes the post-war years and refers to 1946 as the date of Miss Brodie's death from cancer. Thus, within a short narrative, Muriel Spark manages to telescope the events of some sixteen years.

The many references to the important events of this period are helpful to the creation of the main characters. As a teacher Miss Brodie encourages her girls to take a lively interest in contemporary culture. She takes them to see the ballerina Anna Pavlova and mentions actresses like Sybil Thorndike and Fay Compton who were popular and well known during the 1930s. There are also references to the prime ministers of the period – Stanley Baldwin and Ramsay MacDonald.

Jean Brodie is also fascinated by fascism, especially by the autocratic rule of Benito Mussolini in Italy. Her admiration stems partly from her liking for Italian culture and from the holidays she spends in the country. Partly, too, she regards fascism as a forward-looking political philosophy which seems to be very different from the forces of reaction she finds at every turn in Britain. She is also an admirer of Roman civilisation.

It could be said that Miss Brodie's liking for fascism mirrors both her own sense of educational duty and her own sense of destiny, but she is not a simple ideologue. On the contrary, her admiration is simple-minded in that she only likes the sense of order which fascism has brought to Italy and is only prepared to admit that Hitler was 'rather naughty'. At no time does she show any awareness of the evils perpetrated by fascism and only wants to regard it as a force for good.

She is also selective abut her admiration. Although she appreciates the black-shirted followers of Mussolini, she dislikes the Girl Guides and is contemptuous of the school's aim to foster team spirit. Also, as a rigid Scots presbyterian she dislikes Catholicism, the religion of Italy, and when she meets the Pope she makes much of the fact that she refused to kiss his ring but merely moved her lips above it.

At the end of the novel her leanings towards fascism are the cause of her downfall. When Sandy betrays her she tells the headmistress Miss Mackay that although she cannot be sacked on grounds of sexual impropriety she can be caught on the subject of politics. Earlier, Sandy has discovered that Miss Brodie encouraged a new girl, Joyce Emily Hammond, to run off to the Spanish Civil War to fight for General Franco's Falangists. As it is 1938, with the war against Hitler only a year away, Miss Mackay has every reason to sack Miss Brodie.

In the same way that the novel is set in an identifiable city, Edinburgh, Muriel Spark makes good use of the historical and political background. Jean Brodie is a product of that period: she lost her fiancé during the First World War and as a result is a spinster. But she also has an enquiring, if only half-educated, mind and she is fascinated by the events of her day. This leads her to love Italy and to admire fascism and in both passions lie the key to her eventual downfall.

---

(13) Compare and contrast the double lives led by Miss Brodie and Sandy Stranger.

Both Jean Brodie, the teacher, and Sandy Stranger, one of her pupils, lead double lives throughout the period of the novel. Partly this is a self-protective device to hide aspects of their lives which might otherwise be painful, and, partly, it allows them to give full rein to their imaginations.

Miss Brodie's surname is a clue to her double life. She reminds her pupils that she is a descendant of William Brodie, the notorious Edinburgh deacon who was an upright citizen by day yet transformed himself into a robber by night. He lived in Edinburgh during the eighteenth century and was eventually unmasked by the authorities and hanged on a gallows of his creation. By giving Miss Brodie this lineage, Muriel Spark is under-lining the fact that the principal character in her novel also leads a double life.

At an early stage in the novel Miss Brodie reveals evidence of her double life. While teaching her class a history lesson she introduces the story of Hugh Carruthers, her fiancé who died during the last days of the First World War. Although from a poor background, Hugh was an artist and a poet. His death has given Miss Brodie the impetus to devote herself to her girls while she is still in the prime of life.

However, as the novel progresses, Hugh's story also changes and Sandy notices that Miss Brodie seems to be changing it to suit her own needs. This provides a humorous point of connection between the two characters. Sandy and her friend Jenny write a romantic fantasy about Hugh which combines many of the elements of Miss Brodie's real-life relationship with the music teacher Mr Lowther. Thus, both teacher and pupil are joined together in helping to create one aspect of Miss Brodie's imagined other existence.

There is also a serious and less pleasing side to Miss Brodie's tendency to lead one life and create another. She teaches her girls about the importance of romantic love and reinforces the message with references to romantic art and literature yet she refuses to have an affair with Teddy Lloyd because he is married and a Roman Catholic. (On the other hand she sleeps with the dreary Gordon Lowther who is hardly the model of a romantic hero.) This conservatism sits badly with her own scorn for the prime minister Stanley Baldwin and his political message, 'safety first'.

Later, she attempts to encourage one of her pupils, pretty Rose Stanley, to have a love affair with Teddy Lloyd. In this way her surrogate will be her proxy in a relationship which she has refused to enter. This desire to manipulate other people's lives, to play God, is one reason why Sandy eventually turns against her. There is also something preposterous about Miss Brodie's dislike of Catholicism and her admiration for all things Italian.

On the other hand, Sandy Stranger's tendency to lead a double life is more serious and potentially more dangerous. From an early age she escapes from the dull routines of everyday life by engaging in imagined conversations with literary characters such as Mr Rochester from Charlotte Brontë's novel *Jane Eyre* or Alan Breck Stewart from Robert Louis Stevenson's novel *Kidnapped*. She also imagines speaking to the Lady of Shalott from the poem by Alfred, Lord Tennyson.

The unknown narrator of the novel explains that Sandy engages in these activities to prevent herself getting bored, but there is more to the conceit than a desire to escape into an imaginative world of her own creation. Sandy is a genuine outsider, the one member of the group of girls who understands Miss Brodie's methods. In time this ability to watch and observe leads her to become Miss Brodie's confidante and at one stage she is even described as a 'spy'. Like Miss Brodie, her surname – Stranger – is also a clue to her function within the novel.

In time, as she matures, Sandy stops her imaginary conversations but she remains a divided personality to the very end. Although she is closest to Miss Brodie in character and personality, she betrays her because she disapproves of her methods and, thereby, finds herself both judge and executioner. Having done that she turns to Catholicism – the very religion which Miss Brodie detests – and, later still, she becomes a nun. In this new existence her name is Sister Helena of the Transfiguration which is an apposite description of her own position. Sandy Stranger, an outsider as a girl, has become S)ster Helena, a nun who is never at peace with herself. Our final glimpse of her shows her gripping the bars of her cell, a desperate gesture from an equally desperate and unsettled character.

There is, therefore, a vital difference between the lives led by these two characters. While Miss Brodie remains blissfully unaware of the contradictions in her life, they are evident to Sandy Stranger. Not only does she realise the extent of Miss Brodie's manipulations but it provides her with the excuse to betray her to the school's headmistress, Miss Mackay.

Part 5

Suggestions for further reading

Background reading

BOLD, A.: *Modern Scottish Literature*, Longman, London, 1983.

ROYLE, T.: *The Mainstream Companion to Scottish Literature*, Mainstream, Edinburgh, 1993.

SPARK, M.: *Curriculum Vitae* (autobiography), Constable, London, 1992. It is well worth reading this, as it will give you many insights into the way Muriel Spark has distilled her writing from her real life.

SPARK, M.: 'What Images Return', in MILLER, K. (ED.), *Memoirs of a Modern Scotland*, Faber & Faber, London, 1970.

Critical studies of Muriel Spark

BOLD, A. (ED.): *Muriel Spark: An Odd Capacity for Vision*, Vision Press, London, 1984.

BOLD, A.: *Muriel Spark*, Methuen, London and New York, 1986.

KEMP, P.: *Muriel Spark*, Paul Elek, London, 1974.

KERMODE, F.: *Modern Essays*, Fontana, London, 1971. Discusses Spark's early fiction, pp. 267–83.

LODGE, D.: *The Novelist at the Crossroads*, Routledge & Kegan Paul, London, 1971. Discusses *The Prime of Miss Jean Brodie*, pp. 119–44.

MALKOFF, K.: *Muriel Spark*, Columbia University Press, New York and London, 1979.

MASSIE, A.: *Muriel Spark*, Ramsay Head Press, Edinburgh, 1979.

STUBBS, P.: *Muriel Spark*, Longman for the British Council, Harlow, 1973.

Some early books by Muriel Spark

The Comforters (novel), Macmillan, London, 1957; Penguin, Harmondsworth, 1963.

Memento Mori (novel), Macmillan, London, 1959; Penguin, Harmondsworth, 1961.

The Ballad of Peckham Rye (novel), Macmillan, London, 1960; Penguin, Harmondsworth, 1963.

The Girls of Slender Means (novel), Macmillan, London, 1963; Penguin, Harmondsworth, 1966.
Collected Stories I, Macmillan, London, 1967.
Collected Poems I, Macmillan, London, 1967.
Doctors of Philosophy (play), Macmillan, London, 1963.

The author of these notes

TREVOR ROYLE is the Associate Editor of *Scotland on Sunday* and a former Literature Director of the Scottish Arts Council. He has also served as Chairman of the Society of Authors in Scotland and is a board member of the Scottish National Dictionary Association. Amongst his most recent books are *In Flanders Fields; Scottish Poetry and Prose of the First World War* (1990), *Glubb Pasha: The Life and Times of Sir John Bagot Glubb of the Arab Legion* (1992), *The Mainstream Companion to Scottish Literature* (1993) and *Irregular Soldier: The Biography of Orde Wingate* (1995). He is currently working on a history of the end of the British Empire in Africa.